True to Life

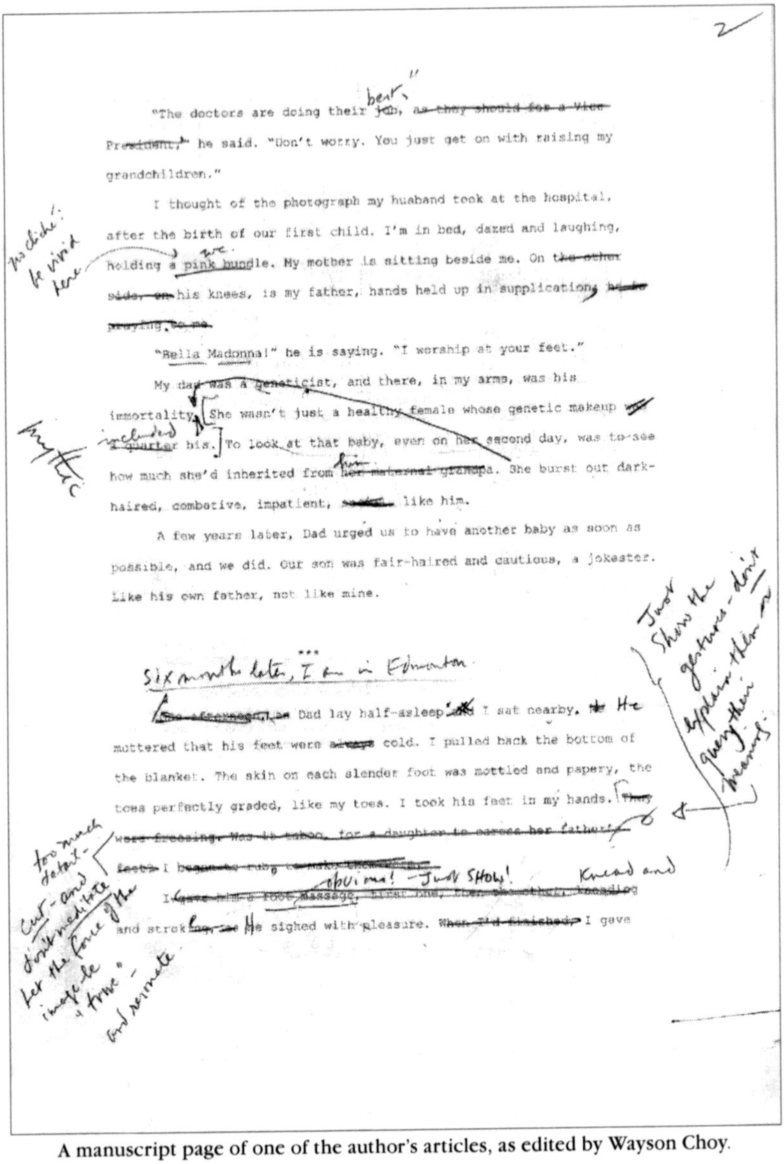

"The doctors are doing their ~~job~~ best," ~~as they should for a Vice~~
~~President,~~" he said. "Don't worry. You just get on with raising my
grandchildren."

I thought of the photograph my husband took at the hospital,
after the birth of our first child. I'm in bed, dazed and laughing,
holding a pink bundle. My mother is sitting beside me. On ~~the other~~
~~side, on~~ his knees, is my father, hands held up in supplication ~~to me~~
~~praying, to me.~~

[handwritten margin: no cliché. He vivid here]

[handwritten: are]

"Bella Madonna!" he is saying. "I worship at your feet."

My dad ~~was a geneticist~~, and there, in my arms, was his
immortality. [She wasn't just a healthy female whose genetic makeup
~~included~~ a quarter his.] To look at that baby, even on her second day, was to see
how much she'd inherited from ~~her maternal grandpa~~ him. She burst out dark-
haired, combative, impatient, ~~sudden~~ like him.

[handwritten margin: hmm! etc.]

A few years later, Dad urged us to have another baby as soon as
possible, and we did. Our son was fair-haired and cautious, a jokester.
Like his own father, not like mine.

Six months later, I am in Edmonton.

~~One afternoon, as~~ Dad lay half-asleep ~~and~~ I sat nearby. ~~He~~ He
muttered that his feet were ~~always~~ cold. I pulled back the bottom of
the blanket. The skin on each slender foot was mottled and papery, the
toes perfectly graded, like my toes. I took his feet in my hands. ~~They~~
~~were freezing. Was it taboo, for a daughter to caress her father's~~
~~feet? I began to rub~~ Obvious! — Just SHOW! Knead and
~~I gave him a foot massage, first one, then the other,~~ ~~kneading~~
and strok~~ing, as~~ He sighed with pleasure. ~~When I'd finished,~~ I gave

[handwritten margin right: Just show the gestures — don't explain them — query their meaning]

[handwritten margin left: too much detail — Cut — and don't immediately let the force of the "implicate" "true" and reinstate]

A manuscript page of one of the author's articles, as edited by Wayson Choy.

True to Life

*Fifty Steps to Help You
Tell Your Story*

B E T H   K A P L A N

Toronto and New York

Published in 2014 by
BPS Books
Toronto and New York
www.bpsbooks.com
A division of Bastian Publishing Services Ltd.

ISBN 978-1-927483-90-9 (paperback)
ISBN 978-1-927483-91-6 (ePDF)
ISBN 978-1-927483-92-3 (ePUB)

Cataloguing-in-Publication Data available from Library and Archives Canada.

Cover: Gnibel
Cover illustration: Alanna Cavanaugh
Text design and typesetting: Tannice Goddard

Printed by Lightning Source, Tennessee. Lightning Source paper, as used in this book, does not come from endangered old-growth forests or forests of exceptional conservation value. It is acid free, lignin free, and meets all ANSI standards for archival-quality paper. The print-on-demand process used to produce this book protects the environment by printing only the number of copies that are purchased.

❧

To all the writers who have entranced and inspired me from the earliest days of my life: the picture book, children's book, and young adult writers, the novelists, the short story writers, the playwrights, the poets.

And most of all, the non-fiction writers with their true-to-life stories: the memoirists and biographers and travel writers, and the essayists who speak straight to us about what matters.

To two writers in particular: Patsy Ludwick, who helped launch this book, and Wayson Choy, who helped launch this author.

To my students, who teach me.

And to Eli, who is two and really likes books, which means he's another of the blessed ones who will always have company.

❧

It all comes in a package,
Unlike a commodity
I'm me. Unique,
And you don't have to like me.

I'm serious. Everything I do
Is an assertion of who I am,
And if I bewilder you
It's because I vary.

Nevertheless I'm a gift
Offered with no conditions
To you. Since I damn well exist
You do too.

MILTON ACORN

Used with permission of Mary Hooper and the estate of Milton Acorn.

Contents

PUT ON YOUR EDITOR'S HAT

SOME RECOMMENDED MEMOIRS

Introduction

Some years ago I went to a writing workshop in Siena, Italy, run by Toronto's School for Writers at Humber College. My reasons for going to one of the world's most sublime countries were obvious—pasta and paintings, for a start. I wasn't sure, though, why I'd submit my writing to a workshop when I myself had been teaching writing at a university for more than a decade. I'd also recently finished my first book, a massive biography of my great-grandfather who'd once been known as the Jewish Shakespeare, and at that moment, a respected New York agent was looking for a publisher.

For my presentation to the workshop, I selected the book's first fifteen pages, which introduced both the old man and me, his great-granddaughter. But as I sent them off, I thought, "I have an agent. I don't need to work on this."

And yet I knew I did. It was on those few pages that Wayson Choy, the extraordinary workshop leader, novelist, memoirist, and master teacher, would base his comments. And when it was my turn to be critiqued, he let me have it—right, as my dad would say, in the kishkas. The tender bits, deep inside.

"Beth's pages are journalism, not creative non-fiction," Wayson announced to my classmates, who had all read my piece. "There are two voices. Every so often we hear the heartbreaking, personal, honest daughter and great-granddaughter. And then she vanishes into the objective journalist again. Where's the story? Where's the dirty laundry? Where are the hot bits? Without these, all we've got are details on a tombstone."

He turned to me. "Where are you? Where's your father?"

"But," I said, "this isn't about me or my father. It's about the Jewish Shakespeare." I burst into tears.

"As far as I can see," said Wayson, "it's also about a woman struggling to know her father by learning about his family. You lack courage to tell the whole story, the real story. Your view is buried by no's from your father, your mother, yourself. You're being a good child, living in fear."

He came close to me, intent. "You must risk telling what is true. If you don't tell the story truthfully, it isn't worth telling."

I felt like I'd been plowed under by a tractor. A wise, helpful, ten-ton tractor.

"Cut the psychological umbilical cord," the teacher said to the class, as I patted my eyes. "The duty of the living is to heal the living. The dead owe us their stories. They can set us free."

WAYSON HAD SENSED that I was ready to hear his tough words, and he was right. He'd cracked open a great vulnerability: My charismatic, brilliant, sometimes terrifying father, who'd been dead for fifteen years, was haunting me.

The class broke for lunch, and the others vanished discreetly, leaving me on my own. Dazed, I walked into the perfumed air of Siena in October. I wandered to the magnificent Piazza del Campo—the town's central plaza—and sat outside at a trattoria, gazing at the great bowl of the open arena in front of me. Crowds of citizens and tourists were walking by or sprawled on the ground, warming their limbs on the ancient stones.

And I invited my father—the ghost of my father—to join me. He and I sat side-by-side, our faces to the sky. How he loved travel, Italy, the hot sun. How he loved the black espresso I was drinking for us both. As we sat, he was devouring the scene, wanting everything: to eat all the food, to sleep with all the beautiful women, to argue with all the men.

And I was looking at the miracle of human creativity—the graceful medieval buildings of Tuscany, beautiful in a way nothing in North America is beautiful. "I'm not hungry like Dad was hungry," I thought. "I'm not fearful as he was fearful. I have hungers and fears, but they're not the same as his."

I turned to him, the great force I loved profoundly even when he caused me pain. Such intelligence, humour, and love in the eyes; incomprehensible fury, too.

"Dad," I said, "I don't want to protect you anymore."

"Write what you need to write, bella Pupikina," he replied, using my favourite nickname, a mixture of Italian and Yiddish. "I'm proud of you."

And I knew he was.

I FINISHED THE bitter coffee and walked to the bell tower in the Piazza. Because it had started to rain, I was the last person admitted to climb the four hundred steps to the top. Once there, I stood alone, enraptured, before the timeless sweep of the city: the dark red roofs, the golden Tuscan stone, the grey-green hills and olive groves beyond. In the sky above the marble-streaked clouds, there for me alone, was a rainbow. The shimmering arc was such a cliché, it made me laugh out loud.

I climbed down and went back to class. That evening, I started to rewrite.

MY CREATIVE STRUGGLES didn't end miraculously that day. Writing well is hard, and so is telling the truth. But after Siena, as I worked, I was aware of, and trying to silence, a critical negativity I myself had put in place.

"Do not be stopped!" I could hear Wayson saying. "Do not be defeated."

4

When scoffers say writing cannot be taught, I think of my encounter with Wayson Choy. Talent cannot be taught, but methodology and craft can. A boot in the butt at the right time is a big help, too. For years after we met, Wayson continued to be my writing teacher. While I taught others to show, not tell, or to open up and "unpack" the vital secrets in their stories, he scoured my own work and pointed out where I was telling, not showing, where I was still hidden and closed. He also became my teaching colleague, passing on new ways to guide students along the path to good writing.

Now I WANT to share what I've learned from Wayson, from my own writing, and from my twenty-year teaching practice. Hence this book, which is designed to give you a great deal of information in a tight space—fifty short, compact lessons to help you on the journey to becoming a writer.

The focus is primarily memoir and personal essay, but most of the points hold true for any kind of writing, including fiction.

I hope these steps inspire your own creative and personal epiphanies. Italy, espresso, and rainbow optional. Boot in the butt, however, a given.

PUT ON YOUR
WRITER'S HAT

I

Believe in your stories and your right to tell them

❧

Everyone has a story worth telling, a saga worth listening to. Have you ever been bored somewhere when the dull-looking stranger nearby opened up and began to talk? I can still hear the man beside me on the plane who'd just been diagnosed with multiple sclerosis and was afraid for his children; the woman at a party who dressed heterosexual men in women's clothing for a living. ("They all think they have great legs," she told me.) Flannery O'Connor famously said that anyone who gets through childhood has enough to write about for the rest of time. We all contain a universe of stories.

But which ones to write down and which to share with others? And who would be interested in your stories?

Who cares if you write or not? Don't you have something more useful to do than fiddle around in your own head? Who the hell do you think you are, anyway?

I remember a young student, Grace, who worked hard to write well but every week read us pieces swimming in sweetness. She wrote nothing personal or risky, just generalizations about togetherness and, one week, a homily about 9/11. We could not convince her to speak in her own voice and be honest about her own truths.

On the last day of class, she rushed in, breathless and apologetic. She hadn't had time to write that week, she said, and so had just dashed something off. She was sure it was stupid and mundane.

And then she read. She told us her older sister was a drug addict whose two small children were about to be taken away and put up for adoption. Grace wanted to adopt them. She had found a job in day care, and the summer before she'd volunteered at an orphanage in Romania, a gruelling experience. She hoped her dedication and expertise would convince the authorities she'd be a responsible caretaker for her nephews.

"I'm going in front of the judge tomorrow," she said. "I'd pass out from fear, except that I love those kids so much."

We were so surprised and moved that for a moment no one knew what to say.

Crestfallen, Grace said, "I knew it was terrible. I'm, like, the most boring person on earth."

And we rushed to tell her how riveted we'd been by her treatise on the power of blood ties. I hope she believed us. I hope the judge believed her.

When we tell of the things we care about most deeply, when we dare to write with courage and honesty in our own clear voices, we can mesmerize an audience, as Grace did. We all have powerful, important stories. But sometimes we don't know what they are, and we don't know how to tell them.

What stories do you tell the stranger sitting next to you on the plane? What are the big stories stored in your head and heart? Is it time to write them down?

Whoever you are, no matter how lonely,
the world offers itself to your imagination,
calls to you like the wild geese, harsh and exciting—
over and over announcing your place
in the family of things.

MARY OLIVER

2

Allow yourself to begin

What makes a writer? Simply, the need to process thought and experience by putting words on a page, and the discipline to sit until the work is down, reworked, and finished. And something more: not just the courage, but the craft and technical skill to make the words meaningful to others, whether they find an audience right away or not.

In Amsterdam, in 1942, just before the Nazis drove her family into hiding, a thirteen-year-old girl was given a plaid notebook for her birthday. Anne Frank made sense of the insanity of global conflict and the hardships of her daily life by scribbling in that notebook. She wrote with the passion, clarity, and insight of a born writer; she edited her work, too, with an eye to publication.

Anne Frank changed the world. When the diary was discovered and published after her death in Bergen-Belsen, her words forever altered the way the world looked at the Nazi atrocities of the Second World War. Six million Jewish men, women, and children died in the Holocaust, but one of them was a child with a name, a face, and a wise, unforgettable voice. In 1999, *Time* magazine published its selection of the "Hundred Most Influential People of the Twentieth Century." Along with great world leaders, scientists, warriors, movie stars, and artists, the list included a girl shut in an attic with a notebook.

A writer is someone who needs to write, who finds a way to get the words onto paper, and who works to make those words tell a living story. And sometimes a writer is a person who changes the world with words.

Do you feel that this definition leaves you out? What would it take for you to consider yourself a writer? Untamed Margaret Atwoodesque hair? A garret in Paris? A literature prize? If you set the bar too high, you'll never start. How about seeing your name in print somewhere, above or below a piece of your writing? Would that be enough? We'll work on that.

In the meantime, how about a notebook full of your words? They're written, aren't they? So didn't a writer write them? **Don't cut yourself off and count yourself out.** Every writer has to start somewhere.

CBC Radio host Eleanor Wachtel interviews writers from around the world for her superb program *Writers and Company*, a must for anyone interested in literature (broadcast on Sunday afternoons on CBC Radio One; available as a podcast at cbc.ca). She was once asked what, if anything, the hundreds of writers she has talked to have in common. She replied, "They all define themselves as outsiders."

Haven't you always been something of an outsider? So you fit the bill. And if you don't define yourself as an outsider, you fit another bill.

Enough with the self-doubt. You're going to write. Let's get to work.

The writer must be universal in sympathy and an outcast by nature; only then can he see clearly.

JULIAN BARNES

Why shouldn't you have the right to become who you are?

WAYSON CHOY

3

Try keeping a journal

How about diving into your own plaid notebook?

I have been a diarist for more than fifty years; my past is stored in boxes under my bed. I began at age nine with a gold Five Year Diary with lock and key; in my teens I wrote in stacks of Hilroy scribblers, and, later, in dignified grown-up Italian, French, and Korean notebooks. Now my chronicles are instantly transmitted to the world through my blog. But sometimes I still write my private inner thoughts on my computer, print them, delete them, and store the printed pages in a binder. Why not simply save the entries on the computer in a locked diary file? Because my diaries have to be on paper, as they have been for so long. Maybe yours don't.

A journal is a way of keeping yourself company on the page. Why don't you try it? **Find time on a regular basis to talk to yourself on paper or screen.** Let ideas, thoughts, and feelings flow; don't reread or fiddle, just keep writing. Note events, dreams, fancies, ideas, fears, jokes. Allow yourself to laugh, rage, muse, and cry. Tell the truth; don't edit or censor. No one is reading but you. **Please make sure no one is reading but you.** When those you live with know you are keeping a diary, they're interested; the most ethical people have a way of finding private writing and "happening" to read it. Why not? It's gripping stuff. But it's your stuff, and you should have the right to say what you want without censure, no matter how nasty, strange, or "unlike you" it may be. You don't want your housemates to see your writing and be offended or hurt. So keep your journals away from prying eyes in a locked computer file or, for those on paper, in a safety deposit box, a small office safe, even the trunk of your car. Seriously.

I found out the hard way that ensuring privacy is not so easy. To make certain none of my diaries from a troubled time would fall into the wrong hands, I locked them in a strongbox with a padlock. My fourteen-year-old daughter found the box and pried it open with a crowbar. A crowbar! She thought it was her brother's and wanted to know his secrets. Instead she found mine. Now my private pages are camouflaged in an innocuous binder among many others on the highest shelf.

Some say there are certain stories they just don't want to write down, thinking that if the tales remain untold, hidden away, perhaps they'll vanish, or perhaps they didn't even happen. Whereas, if the stories are brought into the light, they must be true. Take it from me: Buried stories will go on haunting you. Write them down. Remember, they don't have to be sent out into the world, now or ever. Keep them to yourself if you want, but get them on paper. Begin by telling the important, difficult stories to yourself, bit by bit, in a diary.

You don't have to write every day. In this age of electronic communication, we share our private thoughts constantly with correspondents around the world; my e-mails to best friends, as well as my blog, are now like a journal. But every so often I have to sit and write just for myself. Write for yourself. Because in the end you are writing for no one else. You are writing to explore your own mind, to record your thoughts, to find out who you are and what you think.

There are no rules for journals. Just pick up a loose-leaf binder or a tiny laptop. Find a magnificent Italian hardcover notebook—unless you'll be intimidated by its expensive beauty. Buy a cheap drugstore scribbler—unless you only feel inspired by soft, rich paper under your hands. **Try different containers for your private words until you find the one that feels right.**

To find inspiration for your diary, read a famous person's. Read Anne's. Read accounts of daily life in Samuel Pepys, intimate erotic life in Anaïs Nin, a writer's life in Virginia Woolf. Check out a good journal compilation (some are listed at the end of this book).

Incidentally, there's a clause in my will about the fate of my diaries. That's something to think about if you have personal writing lying around. My children will need to decide together what to do with all those confidential words. If they want to dance around shredding notebooks, they may; if they want to find a publisher and let all my secrets loose, they may. I won't care; I'll be dead. But this is a decision you should make about your private writing while you're around.

Don't burn anything, *please*. I've heard many stories of diarists who burned journals or letters and later wished they hadn't. If you need to put them away for a while, hide them somewhere safe, like treasure—because they are treasure. Remember, one day they might be invaluable for research. Don't destroy them irrevocably; leave that for your descendants.

Travelling in Cape Breton one fall, I stayed in a bed and breakfast in a farmhouse once owned by the landlord's grandfather. Beside my four-poster bed was a faded old book that turned out to be the first owner's diary. As I lay in bed in the late 1900s reading the faded little notebook, I heard the impassive voice of a farmer in the late 1800s tell about his crops, the weather, the birth of animals, the purchase of a new buggy, and, almost indecipherable behind the flat scrawl of the words, the death of a child. That farmer's century-old diary was a gift to me. Perhaps one day your diary will be a gift, enlightening readers about life in your time.

We write journals to dig down deep into our own souls—to send a message to the future and shine a light into the past.

Everybody needs his memories. They keep the wolf of insignificance from the door.

SAUL BELLOW

Freedom is the giddy promise of writers' journals: freedom to try things out, to write clumsy sentences when no one is looking, to be prejudiced, even stupid. No one can expect to write well who will not first take the risk of writing badly. The writer's notebook is a safe place for such experiments.

PHILIP LOPATE

4

Take note

As a writer, you need to pay attention to your thoughts and ideas. They vanish quickly, so grab them on the fly. In addition to the ever-present cellphone, try always to have paper and pen or pencil with you so you can jot things down—for example, file cards that fit in the back pocket of jeans.

Many writers create "daybooks" or scrapbooks of bits and pieces—sayings, postcards, poems. Why don't you start one? **Save not only your own words and ideas but those of others that might inspire you one day.** (As many do, I collect *New Yorker* cartoons, including a favourite by the wonderful George Booth. A befuddled man sits frozen at his typewriter while all around him sprawl a dozen dogs. His impatient wife stands in the doorway. "Write about dogs!" she says.)

Keep a pen and paper beside your bed; you never know when your best ideas will sail in. If you're quick, you can also record your most interesting dreams, setting down what is flooding your subconscious at four in the morning. Keep a notebook for jottings in the glove compartment of your car, in your purse or backpack, in a separate file on your computer. As for those scraps of notes on napkins, envelopes, and loose pages, keep track of them by putting them in a binder or file folder so you can find them when you need them. **Learn to file: Keeping track of your research, ideas, and written work is tedious—and invaluable.**

Listen all the time to the voices around you, to vocabulary and turns of phrase; steal them and jot them down. Writers are magpies, taking all that is bright for their own—and disguising it, if necessary.

Of course you should always have a notebook with you when you travel—the perfect time, as you sit on buses, planes, and trains, to keep yourself company with words. All the details of your trip will blur together or even vanish unless you keep notes or a blog. Save your descriptive e-mails from the road; copy them to yourself, too. You could acquire a small voice recorder for the ideas you have while driving or walking on the beach; your phone might be handy for this, too.

Some writing types, including your humble correspondent, have several notebooks: a journal, a travel notebook, a book for jottings and sayings, a book for dreams. Doing this is not self-indulgence. It is learning to pay attention to your own voice and to all the voices around you.

Begin right now. Take paper or a file card and write down something you overheard, noticed, or thought about today. Stick the card in a notebook or scrapbook or file folder and label it. You are beginning to listen to yourself. Your writer's collection has begun.

And remember ... write about dogs.

This is the first, the wildest and the wisest thing I know: The soul is built entirely out of attentiveness.

MARY OLIVER

5

Carve out a creative space

If you've begun to keep a journal and jot down notes, writing on a regular basis, you are getting used to registering the ideas, emotions, and memories in your head and heart, your brain and your gut. You are learning how to transfer them down your arm, through your hand(s), and out onto the page.

It's time to think of the next step. You want to write not just thoughts but stories. Maybe you want to write a memoir or publish some personal essays or put down the family saga so it'll be preserved for the coming generations or get that trip to Bali on paper before you forget ...

You want to become not only a diarist with private thoughts but also a writer with public thoughts. A writer uses special tools. You wouldn't begin to make a bookshelf without a hammer, a measuring tape, a drill. You shouldn't begin to write seriously without thinking about tools to make the job physically possible. The questions you need to answer first are where, when, and how. The place, the time, and the implements.

I've heard that long before Alice Munro dared admit to herself that she was a writer, she sat for hours at the breakfast table and scribbled stories on the backs of bills that had just arrived in the mail. Colette wrote many of her books in bed. You need to make a place, however humble or odd, for your writing self. It doesn't matter where, as long as it affords you physical and psychic space: the local coffee shop, the commuter train on the way to work, or, ideally, at least sometimes, a desk in a room with a door that closes. You will feel freer creatively in a comfortable, encouraging place.

One day in class, a shy, self-deprecating student informed us that she had gone to IKEA, bought the smallest desk they had, and assembled it in a corner of the bedroom. This, she told her husband and kids, was where she would be a writer. It was as big a step toward artistry and independence as she had ever taken. One small desk for writing-kind.

If your job involves writing, you might need to use a spot other than your workspace for creative endeavours. Some, as Sartre and de Beauvoir did, enjoy filling pages in the anonymity and bustle of cafés. In this age of laptops, we're free to set up a kind of office anywhere. Try different spaces and see what works.

I used to think I couldn't be a proper writer because, as a single mother, I was at the centre of constant domestic activity in my household. When a windfall came my way, I rented a tiny office space and discovered I couldn't work there either; it was too isolated, too quiet. Then I read Isaac Bashevis Singer, who won a Nobel Prize for his work in Yiddish. "I think that being disturbed is part of human life," he said. "I have never really written in peace."

I ditched my excuses and just got on with it, sitting at the desk in my home office when I could—which for years was not often—grabbing time as the commotion swirled around me. Maybe my work has suffered. Maybe it has profited.

Carve out your space, and make it work for you.

I feel that art has something to do with the achievement of stillness in the midst of chaos.

SAUL BELLOW

6

Make time

So now you have a writing spot. What about time? Unless you have retired or won the lottery, there are exhausting demands on your days and nights. You have to study for exams, earn a living, raise children, shop, cook, and eat. Where in the midst of all that essential activity are you going to make time for the non-essential task of writing stories? No one is begging you to write. You are the only one who can ensure that your extremely busy life includes time with your notebook. Two hours on Saturday mornings? Twenty minutes every evening? It doesn't have to be a huge commitment at the start. Just enough so you know that there, in your frantic schedule, is the box with "Writing Time" in it.

The prolific Victorian writer Anthony Trollope completed forty lengthy novels and books of stories and essays while holding a full-time job in the post office. He wrote for a few hours before he went to work, producing a thousand words, or four pages, an hour. One morning he finished an entire novel fifteen minutes before he was due to stop writing for the day. He put it to one side, got out a fresh sheet of paper, and began the next, stopping right on time.

What kind of crazy driven man was that? One who completed all those books while holding a full-time job. A single father and businessman I taught found a way, like Trollope, to write when he could: During his coffee and lunch breaks, he scribbled in the solitude of the supply closet or sometimes in his car. (See Step 5.)

If you can be flexible with time, figure out how and when you work best. Some professional writers like to work for many hours in a great burst of energy and then rest; others find that level of concentration impossible and cannot give more than a few hours a day before they're spent. Which are you? Many creative people say first thing in the morning, when the imagination is fresh and fertile, works best. Others prefer night, when rooms and streets are silent.

One study concluded that the optimum times for most brains are from nine to eleven in the morning and from seven to nine at night. Can you clear one of those times once or twice a week or on weekends? If so, be sure to turn off the Internet, put on your answering machine, and resist the howls of family, chores, your day job, e-mail, Twitter, YouTube, and Facebook until your time is up.

Fulltime caregivers, in particular the parents of young children or teens, can find it especially difficult to set aside even an hour or two just for themselves. I tell them—and when my kids were at home, I used to tell myself, without much success—about something I call "beneficial selfishness." Making space for your own needs is healthy, in the long run, for everyone.

"I didn't have time to write this week" is the most frequent excuse I hear from students. Why do we cheat ourselves of vital creative time? Why don't we value the needs of our own voices, our inner selves? Commit to your own creativity.

On the other hand, I've had students so keen to begin writing that they quit their jobs to give themselves time. This can be a mistake. As new retirees sometimes find out, having countless free hours sounds liberating but is actually scary. There's that blank page along with a blank timetable. How to fill both?

If you do have a lot of time and want to write, begin in small increments. Be strict: Allow yourself one or two hours a day, or even just thirty minutes; set a timer and make yourself stop when time is up. Stretch, relax, and do something else. Let yourself be eager to return. You can slowly increase the time once you've got the rhythm. But at the beginning, set the timer: one or two hours at most. And then stop.

Otherwise, with all the time in the world, you risk writing nothing at all.

Look at your agenda and find your time. Write it down now. Let your friends and significant others know when you've scheduled creative work and ask that at those times they leave you alone.

I have a great deal of company in my house; especially in the morning, when nobody calls.

HENRY DAVID THOREAU

Don't wait for the muse. She has a lousy work ethic. Writers just write.

BARBARA KINGSOLVER

7

Choose your tools

A re you a pen person or a computer person? Seriously consider trying both. The rhythm of scratching a pen nib across a piece of paper has been with humanity for many hundreds of years, the speedy bounce of a cursor along a lighted screen for only a few decades. Some believe the ease of word processing has improved speed but not writing content and style. Perhaps you are so used to the responsive hare-like dash of the computer that the old-fashioned technology of the pen makes you feel like a lumbering tortoise. But remember who won the race.

Many writers—J.K. Rowling is one—still write long-hand and transcribe their words onto a computer as their second draft. I strongly recommend that computer junkies try writing first drafts with paper and pen. It's a sane, connected rhythm. And typing that material into the computer affords a whole new view of the work.

After several PCs, my first Mac, stylish white MacZine, became my best friend. I loved her and her silvery replacements MacTruck and FleetwoodMac. But for most first drafts, I still write longhand. I choose my pens carefully —a thick nib, a slender carriage, easy ink flow, and black ink. There are three pots stuffed with pens beside me right now, and pencils, too, newly sharpened. Hemingway did all his first drafts in pencil. Neil Gaiman uses classy Waterman fountain pens. Mmmm.

What about paper? Thick, thin, recycled, lined, unlined? Big yellow pads or pretty French notebooks? If you use a computer, can you write a whole piece without printing, or do you need to print regularly so you can see words on paper? Don't forget all those nifty little devices beloved of paper nuts: erasers, Wite-Out, rulers, paper clips, file folders, Post-it notes, Sharpie markers. Perhaps, at the beginning of the writing process, you could use large sheets of unlined paper and crayons or felt pens, drawing pictures to access another part of the brain. Later, you could make sense of a chaotic manuscript by sticking file cards to the wall or spreading them across the floor or stringing them on a clothesline.

What else might you need? Scanner, hole-punch, bulletin board, backscratcher? Rock collection? Pictures of your family or guru for inspiration—or would that be too distracting? Music? Noise-cancelling earphones?

And then there's one of the most important tools of all: a wastepaper basket or recycling bin. Use yours fearlessly. I have in my office an inspiring picture of the great *New Yorker* essayist E.B. White writing in his country cabin. There is nothing in the room where he works except a plain plank desk and bench, a manual typewriter, pencils—and a very large barrel for his rejected pages.

Make the effort to choose the right tools. This is the fun part—strapping on your tool belt and getting ready to work. Aldous Huxley, asked how to become a novelist, replied, "The first thing is to buy quite a lot of paper, a bottle of ink, and a pen. After that you merely have to write."

After you learn to write, your whole object is to convey everything, every sensation, sight, feeling, place and emotion to the reader. To do this you have to work over what you write. If you write with a pencil, you get three different sights at it ... First when you read it over; then when it is typed you get another chance to improve it, and again in the proof. Writing it first in pencil gives you one-third more chance to improve it ... It also keeps it fluid longer so that you can better it easier.

ERNEST HEMINGWAY

8

Grant yourself solitude

℘

Pens, computers, desks: These things are relatively easy
to come by. Difficult for many of us to find is the stillness of mind and surroundings needed for creative effort—
peace, and, at least sometimes, quiet. Ideally, we writers
have regular time alone, in silence. We need quiet to hear
the voice inside. We need that solitary time to sit and look
out the window and drift. Writing is one of the only jobs in
the world—inventing is another—for which part of the job
description is "Must love being alone for hours, mulling."
This use of time is hard to explain to sensible folk who are
not artists: You're just sitting there? Yes. For us, just sitting
there is work, too.

That time musing, staring at a spot on the wall, pacing, gazing blankly out the window, and then picking up pen or setting fingers to keyboard and beginning to scribble— that time is vital. You don't have to justify the seeming lack of activity. If possible, mull in your alone and quiet moments, but remember that Isaac Bashevis Singer rarely wrote in peace. What matters is to make time for mulling and then for writing. You can do these things in a playground if you're focused. For some it's easier, for others scarier, to be alone in silence.

As you mull, remember that the blank page in front of you, waiting for your imprint, is an intimidating sight for *all* writers. Don't be put off. Here are some ideas to give your mulling direction.

Right now, make a list of ten things that touch, obsess, and haunt you: your passions, your fears, the things you believe in most. Without thinking, jot notes about some of them. Eventually, try to write about all of them.

Write the words on your list, and also words from the following exercise, on pieces of paper and fold them. Now set a stopwatch or clock or the alarm on your phone, pick one of the papers, and write, for exactly five minutes, about the word you see. Don't think, don't stop, and don't take your pen off the page for five minutes.

When the five minutes are up, immediately pick another piece of paper and write about that word. Do this three, four, five times. Always stop at the end of five minutes. Don't reread. Put the work away and look later.

You'll be amazed—allow yourself to be amazed. Grant yourself mulling time. That's when your raw material will float to the surface.

It's a constant struggle to find the right balance between solitude and society and I don't think anyone ever does.

EDMUND WHITE

Loneliness is the poverty of self. Solitude is the richness of self.

MAY SARTON

SUGGESTED TOPIC LIST

Just pick one and start. Don't stop for five or ten or even, eventually, twenty minutes. What images do these words bring up?

Colours: green, blue, yellow, black, pink, orange, brown, white, silver, gold.

Seasons: spring, fall, winter, summer.

Holidays: Thanksgiving, Christmas, Hanukkah, Valentine's Day, etc.

Time: evening, morning, night, noon, dusk, dawn.

What I knew. What I didn't know. In five years, I …

First kiss. A good habit. A bad habit.

A neighbour, a foreigner, a best friend, a sibling, a coward, a hero, an enemy, the black sheep.

Dancing, leaving, running (away/to/just because).

Helplessness, a disguise, a vacation, an embarrassment.

List your favourite words. Write about one of them.

Look out the window for five minutes. Write about what you see.

List your five best and five worst teachers. Write about one of them.

Imagine your ideal writing circumstances. Write about them.

List the things you consider taboo. Which can you write about? Start. I dare you.

Something you've lost. Something you want to do before you die. The words that changed your life. The turning point.

Your house is on fire; your family, pets, photo albums, and personal papers are safe. You grab the next most important thing and run. What is it? Why that thing?

Actress and writer Marlo Thomas compiled a fascinating
book called *The Right Words at the Right Time*, in which
celebrities tell the story of the words that changed their
lives. Diane Sawyer the broadcast journalist remembered
her father's questions to her after university, when she had
no idea what to do next: "What is it you love?" he asked.
"Where is the most adventurous place you could do it? And
are you certain it will serve other people?" Can you answer
those questions? Try.

9

Develop a routine

e᷾

It may be hard for me to convince you that you need routine. Boring routine—who wants to do the same thing
regularly, at the same time, like old Anthony Trollope? We
have an image of artists—painters, musicians, writers—as
free spirits who live spontaneous, unfettered lives.

Many are and do. But if they want to get anything
created and completed, no matter how wild and free they
are, they need discipline, and discipline generally involves
routine. That means a time when getting down to work is
so automatic, it doesn't even have to be considered. Every
morning, the dancer and choreographer Twyla Tharp gets
into a cab in her pyjamas and goes to work out at the gym.
She doesn't have to make a decision or even think; it's

simply what she does. Stephen King sits at his desk every single morning and doesn't get up until he has written his quota of two thousand words.

You don't need that kind of fierce daily discipline to have a writing routine. Just knowing that, say, two hours every Tuesday night have been set aside for writing will help. Then you fight to keep Tuesday nights automatically reserved. It's not duty that brings you to the work; it's anticipation and joy made accessible by routine. "Sorry," you will say. "I'm not free that night to go hear the Rolling Stones." Your friends should know by now: It's Tuesday evening, so you're writing. Maybe next time the Stones will come on another night. And when enough Tuesdays have gone by, you will have a lot of pages.

Note to myself: What a hypocrite! Okay, I admit it: Unless I had a deadline, there is no way, if someone gave me a ticket, that I'd miss the Rolling Stones for work. Let's be realistic about life's ability to interfere with the best-laid plans, and about our need to participate in life if we're going to write about it. I'm talking about the general idea: Make a set time to get your brain in gear and stick to it. If you break your routine in order to see the Stones, find another time that week to do your work. That's all it takes.

And when you are sitting there at your set time, look at the list you've made of your obsessions and loves. Dwell on the stories from your life that are important to you. Mull. Jot. Begin, bit by bit, to get thoughts and scenes down, in more detail than the pieces in Step 8. Don't worry about shape, grammar, spelling, where they start or end.

Just begin putting into words, one by one, the incidents, scenes, and memories that sit most deeply in your heart. Let the words pour out. When you have some pages on one subject, put them away, and the next time you sit down to write, begin on another. Don't reread or rework. Just get started each time and let the pages pile up.

Stacks of pages turn into works of literature. That's how books are made.

You try to sit down at approximately the same time every day. This is how you train your unconscious to kick in for you creatively.

ANNE LAMOTT

We are what we repeatedly do. Excellence, then, is not an act but a habit.

ARISTOTLE

IO

Preserve your family stories

Think of the people in your family who know the famous family stories. Likely *you* are the person in your family who knows or at least is interested in the family stories. Those stories are your wealth. They help explain who you are and where you came from: the particular heritage and values—and secrets—that were given to you with your mother's milk (or your nanny's bottle of formula). As a writer, you are the family chronicler. One of your most important jobs is to preserve your family's stories, good and bad, before they disappear. If you don't, no one will. This also applies if you are adopted, of course. Perhaps you'll unearth the stories of several families.

"No one talks in my family," people often complain, Sometimes, yes, our relatives will strive to keep the family skeletons locked in the closet, but sometimes they don't talk because we haven't indicated our interest. Have you asked what your dad or granddad did during the war or what your mother's life was like during the Sixties? Have you asked your aunts, uncles, and cousins for their take on the family fables? Or even your own children? You might be astonished by what you learn.

Sometimes family secrets come spilling out, explaining incomprehensible oddities. My dad didn't find out until after his mother's death that when she met the man who would become her husband, she pretended to be eight years younger than she was. She kept those missing years a secret her entire life. This shed light on many mysteries, including why she kept the family away from her sister, who actually *was* eight years younger.

There are books that list questions to help you prompt your speakers. (For example: *Legacy: A Step-by-Step Guide to Writing Personal History* by Linda Spence.) Check out the memory game LifeTimes, the Game of Reminiscence (www.lifetimesthegame.com). Or perhaps, if your relatives are too shy to talk, you could hand over a sheet of questions and ask them to write the answers in their own time. (Don't wait though, before asking again. The forces of resistance and secrecy will work hard against you.) Buy a small voice recorder to set on the table while you are chatting, or, if they prefer, suggest they keep it and entrust their memories to it when they're alone.

Climb up to the attic or down to the basement of your relatives' homes and delve into those decaying trunks, those boxes of dusty photographs and documents. Track down family diaries and letters; I found the letters my parents wrote to each other during the Second World War when they were both barely out of their teens—priceless. Contact your local, regional, or national archives; they have reams of information on file. Enlist your local librarian. Sometimes your search will involve a visit to the old country to find relatives you've never met and to see those legendary places. Book your ticket. Explore the mysteries. What can you lose?

Make the call right now. Phone the person who knows the most about your family and ask a gentle question or two. Get the process of discovery started. And if you are the family repository, begin writing the stories down. There is no time to waste.

"Every time an old person dies," goes the saying, "a library burns down." Make sure the library of your family stories doesn't go up in smoke.

"Remember only this one thing," said Badger. "The stories people tell have a way of taking care of them. If stories come to you, care for them. And

learn to give them away where they are needed.
Sometimes a person needs a story more than food
to stay alive. That is why we put these stories in
each other's memory. This is how people care for
themselves."

BARRY LOPEZ

We cannot resist this rifling around in the past,
sifting the untrustworthy evidence, linking stray
names and questionable dates and anecdotes
together, hanging on to threads, insisting on being
joined to dead people and therefore to life.

ALICE MUNRO

II

Read like a writer

Two activities are essential for the beginning writer. The first—surprise!—is writing. The second is reading—madly, deeply, constantly. You are sucking in words.

Read like a writer. If you find a story or a book that speaks to your deepest soul, read it first as a reader, for the enormous pleasure it brings. And then read it again as a writer. This time, study it closely. How does the writer launch the story, pursue it, end it? What are the tricks of vocabulary, style, or structure you'd like to imitate? Find a few pages you particularly admire and write them out for yourself. Type them on your computer or write them longhand, but as you inscribe the words, analyse how the author achieved something that works so well.

BETH KAPLAN

Make a list of all your best-loved books, including ones from childhood, and tackle them again. Some will seem dated or laboured while others will continue to shine. I think *Charlotte's Web* is one of the best books ever written; E.B. White is one of my favourite writers, and Charlotte the spider is a fine writer herself. I study White's crystalline essays "Death of a Pig" and "Once More to the Lake" (suggestion—read them). How does he achieve that balance of humour and gravity, that delicate precision of vocabulary? He fills me with envy and despair, he's so good. But then he's dead and I'm not, so for now I have a small, and unfortunately temporary, advantage.

Be aware of the activities in your community for readers: writers' festivals where you can put a face to the voices that interest you; readings and book signings at bookstores. In late September, many communities sponsor Word on the Street, a dazzling street festival packed with activities for book lovers. Don't miss it. Read the book review section of your local newspaper and *The New York Times* on Sunday to see what new works are coming out, particularly those in your field of interest. *The New Yorker*, in my opinion, is the best magazine in the world; keeping up with a weekly magazine packed with great reading material is a job in and of itself.

Haunt the local library, one of my preferred destinations; as soon as I hear of a book I'd like to read, I order a copy online, and while in the building, I peruse the New Books display and pile them up. I'm proud to be a junkie of the printed word.

Make a list of all the books you wish you had read. Read them for nourishment and inspiration. Read them again.

One must be drenched in words, literally soaked in them, to have the right ones form themselves into the proper patterns at the right moment.

HART CRANE

When you reread a classic, you do not see more in the book than you did before; you see more in yourself than there was before.

CLIFTON FADIMAN

12

Unleash the "I" word

For some, the "I" word is a problem. In academic and much professional writing, the personal is forbidden. Anecdotes? A warm voice? God forbid, a sense of humour? These frivolities are death to tenure and professional advancement. Writers who have to excise any kind of personal reference will twist their prose into grotesque shapes in order to avoid the skinny, dangerous pronoun "I." *Often one finds that a missing sibling has a negative effect on one's childhood,* they'll say, rather than, *I really missed my brother.* Beware the word "one." Who exactly is "one"? Claim your story.

Other writers hide in the anonymity of the passive voice. *While the thunderstorm raged, the tent was put up and the supper was cooked.* There's a lot going on here, but what can I see? Only nature raging; there's no human being. This is a passive sentence without a subject—a person or a thing performing the deeds described. Compare that with, *While the thunderstorm raged, Dad struggled to pitch the tent and I to heat a can of stew.* A simple change makes an active sentence. Now I can see the rain lashing the sodden campsite and the family battling to get through. I can see you.

Here, bold and unashamed, we are dealing with the self-centred, spotlight-grabbing word "I." This is your story, your life; these are your thoughts, memories, and ideas. You'll have to work hard to write truthful memoir without using the first person singular pronoun again and again. If you really cannot do it, write short stories or novels instead; inventing characters and worlds will free you.

Some writers face additional difficulties in personal writing. I've found in my classes that the male of the species sometimes finds it hard to express or even explore the innermost self. Men write with insight, depth, and humour about their first car or ambitions or grievances but often aren't permitted to have, or do not permit themselves to have, the vulnerability to write with candour about deep-seated feelings. Older writers, from a generation when talking about the self was considered vain, self-indulgent, or vulgar, have trouble, too, as do people from reserved families.

It takes practice and courage for those mentioned above, as well as for people who write professionally— academics, technical experts who put out manuals, or PR, advertising, or fundraising personnel—to begin a sentence with the naked words *I feel* ... Or *I felt* ... Or even, less threateningly, *I thought* ... or *I remember* ... or *When I was six, I had a red Tonka truck that I loved.*

Try it. Yes, it hurts to see your underwear flapping on a public clothesline. Once you get over the shock, though, you'll begin to feel free. If you don't, switch to fiction. What matters is to find the genre that works for you.

Write those beginnings, above, and finish the sentences. The story is from you and about you. Go on; be brave. We want to get to know you. It's time to liberate your inner "I."

Write the words *I remember* ... over and over down a page, and fill in the lines. Go.

Now, just to confuse you, here's a contradictory suggestion: Be careful not to use the first person pronoun too often. Do not start all your sentences with "I." Vary sentence structure, and also make sure you are taking other voices, opinions, and lives into account. You are writing about you, but not only you.

Another issue to consider when beginning to write about your past: The point of view of the "I" you choose determines the voice you use. Will you tell your stories in the voice of a child living through events in the here and now? *I am twelve, and everything my parents do drives me like totally crazy.* In the first-person retrospective voice of an adult looking back? *When I was twelve, I had no respect for my struggling parents.* Or in some combination of both, trying to combine the innocence, energy, and immediacy of a child with the knowledge and wisdom of a grown-up? *My poor struggling parents—when I was twelve, everything about them made me want to scream and run away.* There are advantages and difficulties in each.

Once you've made the choices that will help you master the use of this invaluable pronoun, you're on your way to discovering your voice.

My students are desperate to know: How do I find my voice? How will I know when I've found it? What is my voice? And I reply: Your honest writing voice is the voice you use when you're sitting comfortably with beloved friends, telling them the important stories that have touched you profoundly and that you care about most.

Only better. A clearer, deeper, more confident and concise, more shaped and focused and resonant and articulate you.

That's your voice.

Voice is the knowledge of what you want to say.

ROGER ROSENBLATT

I am grateful to God for giving me this gift, this possibility of developing myself and of writing, of expressing all that is in me.

ANNE FRANK

13

Stand up to the negative voice

W ho cares if you write your stories? No one but you, and sometimes not even you. Writing is hard enough without battling the inner voices that say, "Who do you think you are? You have no talent and nothing to say and are making a fool of yourself, you pathetic, conceited, self-deceiving loser." Sound familiar? (See the list of fears in Step 17.)

Before you put a single word on a page, there is a plot to stop you from writing, and it begins in your own head. There are voices in there: teachers, parents, or siblings who criticized your writing, or just a general spoilsport who doesn't believe in your creative abilities and wants to shut you down.

Kate, a warm, skilled, insightful student writer, amazed us all when she said she hadn't written a word since high school. Her English teacher Mr. Ploux, she told us, had made such fun of her writing that she'd stopped at the age of sixteen and had waited forty years to start again. Now she deeply regretted that waste of time, and her stories tumbled out. Not long after, Kate died suddenly of a brain aneurysm. All the rest of her stories were lost because she'd been silenced by Mr. Ploux.

Ask yourself: How is the world a better place if I am silenced?

The always honest Anne Lamott says that, when she sits down to work, her leering neuroses pull up chairs behind her, around the computer; she can hear them muttering as she writes. Most creative people have to combat their own muttering version of Mr. Ploux. The fact is that we need a critical inner voice that pushes us to improve, but not one that attacks us and shuts us down. We probably cannot make our destructive voices go away, but we can acknowledge their presence and power. We can turn around and say, "I know you're there, but you're not going to stop me. Now leave me alone. I have work to do."

Take time, one day, to sit silently with your eyes closed; relax your shoulders and belly and be aware of your breathing. Start to listen to the sounds in the room, to your heartbeat. Then ask the negative voice in you to speak up. Let it—or them—loose, to say every nasty thing that needs to be said.

Pick up your pen and write down what you hear. Let that petty, judgemental voice have its say fully and openly for five minutes. Time it. Don't stop till the time is up.

Put your pen down, give yourself a shake, breathe deeply, and breathe again, perhaps with your eyes closed. And then listen for another voice. This is you, fierce and forthright, speaking back. Pick up your pen and confront that negative, judgemental voice. Defend your freedom to write. Stand up for yourself. Shout back.

Take ten minutes to battle for your creative rights. If you don't, no one else will.

Believe the second voice. The first, Wayson says, is the voice of the devil.

"Let me block your writing," says the devil. The devil is always there, trying to prevent the truth from coming out.

WAYSON CHOY

If you hear a voice inside you say "You cannot paint" then by all means paint and that voice will be silenced.

VINCENT VAN GOGH

14

Complete your baggy
first draft

❧

You sit staring at the page or the screen and, finally, an idea comes. You begin to write tentatively, then with more confidence. The words start to flow, and the pages take shape. Then you stop and read what you've written, and you want to throw up.

Congratulations! You've done exactly what you're supposed to do. You have written a big fat baggy first draft.

Inexperienced writers think that writing is like laying an egg. You begin by gathering your thoughts, fashioning a nice warm nest. You sit in it, gestate, strain—and voilà, you produce a perfect, shining, egg-shaped piece of writing, a gift to the world all set to go.

But that is the furthest thing from what writing really is: a process, a journey, endless stumbling along a confusing trail. Beginning somewhere, figuring out where you want to go, trying to get there, trying again this way, trying again that way, finishing somewhere and then starting again. This messy, frustrating process is what writing really looks like.

A first draft can and indeed should be awful. In her diary, Virginia Woolf spoke of her first draft as a chaotic handbag into which she threw everything. Try not to edit or stop as your first draft emerges. Let the ideas, thoughts, and scenes pour out until that bag is bulging. You are writing a big fat baggy first draft, wearing your writer's hat (throw all the ideas in) not your editor's hat (weed many ideas out). You can't work with a few tentative lines; you need pages filled with words. When you stop and read your draft, it'll be too terse and constrained or, more likely, way too rambling and long. It'll be full of bad grammar, digressions, and clichés. "All over the place!" you'll say. "So dull. Abysmal."

Forgive yourself. Because now the next part of the work begins: editing, shaping, and improving the baggy first draft.

My first drafts are turgid, unfocused, and lacklustre; they make me think I'm a lousy writer. But I am, I like to think, a good REwriter. Once the first draft is down, I work it over and over into something better—as I'm doing right now, over and over, in this book for you. Some believe getting the first draft out is the hardest part of writing; others love the initial burst of creation and hate the fiddly editing that comes next. Use different techniques to help launch yourself—perhaps drawing or creating mind maps, talking out loud, or making lists and pinning them on the wall.

Writing is more like working with clay than we realize at first; when you've got a lump of raw material, you have to figure out what to do with it, what its final shape should be, and how to get it there. But first, unlike potters or sculptors, you have to produce the raw material yourself, unearthing it onto the page from your own memory, heart, gut, mind, soul.

Delve into your topic, let yourself go, and write a clumsy, bulky, meandering, lousy first draft. Keep writing, keep your writer's hat on, and keep putting in what comes to you until you have enough content to really rewrite. Only then should you put on your editor's hat and begin to redraft, polish, and cut.

When I used to write more at The New Yorker, *there were two or three Polish cleaning women who came in late at night, and I was always afraid that they would find my early drafts and read them to each other, howling with laughter, slapping their brooms against the desks like hockey players do: Ha! He calls himself a writer!*

CALVIN TRILLIN

The first words down are like a block of marble for the sculptor: raw material. The content, or much of it, comes blurting out in the first draft. (Kurt Vonnegut once wrote that this appalling stuff sounds as if it were written by someone named Philboyd Studge.)

JUNOT DIAZ

Let it pour out. Surrender to the story. Write too much so you have something to work with. Don't worry about who will see it; write for yourself. Don't hold back and be discreet. Don't cut yourself off from the story.

WAYSON CHOY

15

Make it matter

 ❧

One of the most common sentiments of beginning memoir writers is, "Who'll be interested in MY story? I'm not famous or interesting." That was the attitude of Grace in Step 1, presenting what she thought was a boring, mundane saga of adoption, which I heard years ago and have never forgotten. Think of high school teacher Frank McCourt, who decided to write a memoir of his Irish childhood. He didn't know if his story would interest anyone, but he had a moving tale and told it well, with detail, dialogue, humour, and skill—and also, considering what a painful story it was, with great compassion for his hapless parents. *Angela's Ashes* became a huge bestseller (suggestion—read it).

The beautiful irony of our work is that the more honest, direct, and passionate we are in telling our own stories, the more our readers will connect to us. This is hard to believe, but it's true, no matter how specific your story is to you, how quirky and unusual. My parents were not alcoholic or Irish, but because McCourt wrote with truth, wit, and daring, I connected on a deep level with the rich humanity in his tale. I don't have a sister, but because Grace told her story with such genuine emotion, I understood something new about the power of the loyalty and concern we feel for our own flesh and blood.

This kind of writing means telling the small story so well, with such focus and heart and skill, that the big story inside it will shine through, though sometimes we don't even know what the big story is. If what you choose to write doesn't matter to you, the writer, it won't matter to your readers. **Trust your important stories and trust your voice to tell them.**

To become better writers, we must work on two fronts. On the one front, we need to summon the courage, depth, and honesty to dig up and recount our most important stories. On the other, we must develop the patience, humility, and dedication to learn the craft and technique of good writing, so that we tell those vital stories well. Craft and courage—that's all you need. If you have lots of courage but no craft, people will be eager to read your honest tales but won't be able to penetrate your prose. If you have lots of craft but no courage, your stories will flow beautifully with rich vocabulary and good structure but may not find readers, because nothing is at risk.

Risk is key. Something must be at stake. Otherwise, why should we care? (Risk is an important topic; see Step 37 and on.)

No tears in the writer, no tears in the reader. No surprise for the writer, no surprise for the reader.

ROBERT FROST

The literary non-fiction writer recreates the narrative so that it becomes resonant. She uses her imagination, but the story is based in fact and emotional truth. She tells her own truth so fully that she enables her readers to remember theirs. An honest story opens others to the possibility of their own humanity. It opens us up, teaches the heart how to manoeuvre and think. We touch a human, visible part of each other when the story rings true.

FROM WAYSON CHOY'S NOTEBOOK

16

Start anywhere

You know the feeling: You have an idea for a story, you're there at your routine time, and now you sit. And sit and sit, and, if you're like me, get up for a snack, do some e-mailing, do a bit of gardening, sit, write a blog post, e-mail some more, get up, do some dishes, inspect your pores in the magnifying mirror, eat some food. And then sit.

Some of those detours are valuable, because while you're messing around in the garden, your mind is messing around with ideas. But sometimes distractions take over because you don't want to start until you've found the exactly perfect first line. And so you sit with pen to paper or fingers on keyboard, waiting for that perfect line to come to you. And until it does, you're paralysed.

Don't wait for it. You can't figure out where your story should actually start until you've finished it. What you have to do is get something on paper, now. **So simply start. Crunch Mr. Ploux under your shoe and put a line down, any line that will propel your story forward, get the thing moving.** Later, when you've moved through the tale, you can go back and see if you've started at the right place or—much more likely—not. It doesn't matter, at first, where you begin.

In the final drafts, the first line or paragraph of your story, or the first page or chapter of your book, is vitally important; the beginning makes a promise the rest of the work is going to keep. You're introducing your narrative drive and your narrative voice, hooking us so we want to go wherever you take us. You need to do this from the outset, as quickly and dramatically as you can.

But you won't know what that first line or paragraph is at the start. **When you sit down to work on a story, begin by flinging ideas into your first draft handbag. You can't come up with the perfect beginning because you don't know where you're going. You won't know what your piece is really about until you've finished a draft or four.**

Unless—a big unless—you are like Alistair MacLeod, the great writer from Cape Breton. He worked by assembling most of the story in his head before writing a word, and then setting down one line at a time, polishing it until it gleamed, and moving on to the next. His work is stunning (suggestion—read it) though his output, not surprisingly, was small.

Most of us could not work in that painstaking way. A writer once talked about his peers as either "ekers or gushers." Which type do you lean toward, the meticulous Alistair MacLeod or the incredibly prolific Joyce Carol Oates? There's no wrong way to work except not to work.

Remember that you'll still need exposition, the facts your readers need to know before embarking with you on your expedition: the context of where, when, who, why. But don't exhaust or confuse them with a series of dense facts at the very beginning. Stage an active scene, dazzle them with voice and story—greet them, welcome them in, make sure they're engaged.

Then inform them of the time, the place, the weather, and why you're hitchhiking to Marrakesh in gumboots.

The first sentence can't be written until the final sentence is written.

JOYCE CAROL OATES

Beginnings are sudden, but also insidious. They creep up on you sideways, they keep to the shadows, they lurk unrecognized. Then, later, they spring.

MARGARET ATWOOD

17

Unblock

I've just given you a series of orders: Try this, don't try that. Maybe by this point you're saying to yourself, "Great. Now my path is becoming clear." Or maybe you're saying, "To hell with this. I'm confused and discouraged, I have no idea what I'm doing, and nothing feels good." And nothing creative comes, sometimes for a day or two, and sometimes for much longer.

Wayson thinks writer's block derives from "personal spiritual wrestling," when a writer is struggling to move to a deeper level or to tell an important story but instead plays it safe and gets stuck. Why don't we ever hear about plumber's block or doctor's block? These professionals may have doubts about their creative or professional abilities, but they can't stop to analyse; they simply get on with routine work. What writers do is so nebulous and so unnecessary to the rotation of the planet that, as we sit alone and mull, it's all too easy for us to think, "Nothing is coming and nothing ever will. This is a meaningless waste of time. I give up."

You are having a crisis of self-confidence. Or you've reached a point where there is something important you need to say but you're afraid to say it. You've hit a wall, you're spinning your wheels, you're stuck in the mud— whatever cliché you use to describe it, the pages are not stacking up.

I've heard a lot of fears—from students reading their most important stories in front of a group of strangers for the first time, or from writers setting out on the long and difficult road to self-knowledge in memoir. They say, "I'm afraid of ..."

- finding out I can't write

- finding out I'm a really good writer (yes, this is a genuine fear)

- finding out I have nothing to say

- finishing a piece

- not finishing a piece

- not finding the right story

- what I'll uncover

- offending others

- being rejected

- being judged

- being found out

- being exposed

- being disillusioned

- looking stupid

- saying too much

- boring myself

- boring other people

- losing my voice

- sounding just like everyone else

- wasting my time

- intimacy

- commitment

- the hard work

Does that list cover it for you? Can you think of something else to fear? Now ask yourself again: Is the world a better place if I am silent?

Some writers stop writing when they reach the end of what Wayson calls "the honeymoon stage" of writing—

when they understand, suddenly, that this is not fun anymore, but hard and painful work. Are you seeing the long stretch of real commitment ahead for the first time? Does it make you want to give up?

Here are a few ideas to get you started again: **Write in the here and now, no more.** On a small piece of paper, describe exactly what's in front of you: desk, table, wall. Look out the window and describe what you see. Start small and expect nothing; write simply, clearly, with lots of sensory detail, and then put it away. Just get the flow down the arm going again, engaging eyes, heart, and mind.

Write a letter. Tell one of your best stories to a real person who adores you, or invent a kind person out there who's eager to read your work. Anne Frank did not in fact write a diary; she wrote letters to an imaginary friend called Kitty. If there is or was no real person in your life who accepts or accepted you without question, invent your own Kitty. The personal voice is freer and more natural in a letter. Try it.

Pick a favourite book, one that speaks to you; select a few of your most loved pages from that book and type or write them out. Copy them exactly, trying to understand how the author worked. Once you find yourself in the flow of that particular mind and voice, continue in your own. Use a master's voice to inspire and encourage you.

If a particular story just will not come, try writing it in the third person with invented names, as if it's fiction. When it's out and down, change it to first person.

Humour helps. I urge students who are nervous before

they read their pieces aloud to use a "generic disclaimer": "I have no idea where this garbage came from" or "This is the worst piece of writing in the history of the world" or "I just tossed this piece of @#$ off on the way here." Maybe you'll feel better if you smack your piece on the head before you start. That's okay. We're listening. Just do not be silenced.

Stop worrying and say something. Go.

Can anything be sadder than work left unfinished?
Yes, work never begun.

CHRISTINA ROSSETTI

Don't romanticise your "vocation." You can either write good sentences or you can't. There is no "writer's lifestyle." All that matters is what you leave on the page.

ZADIE SMITH

18

Check your work
for runways

Some writers like to begin stories with a philosophical reflection, with musing: *There are times in a woman's life when she needs to stop and figure out the man she married. This, I realize now, is one of those times for me. The other day, suddenly, my husband Joey told me he wanted his own bedroom.*

Now imagine flipping through a magazine and reading these first lines: *"Sweetheart," said my husband Joey yesterday, "I love you, but I want my own bedroom."*

The first two lines of the first piece are like a runway for an airplane; the writer is getting revved up before takeoff. These extended starts can also be compared to throat clearing, like a speaker starting a speech. You're warming up, talking to yourself, setting up narrative voice and narrative drive—who is talking and what is happening. But once the story is flying on its own, you can get rid of the devices that got it launched. Chop the philosophizing, musing, meandering runway. Jump into the story, preferably in the middle of the action. You can go back later and clue us in with exposition and set-up.

You've finished your first draft and maybe a few more; you've figured out where the story ends and so, at last, where it starts. Now, when you begin editing and rewriting, make sure you grab your reader at the beginning and don't let go. Don't waste words with a leisurely start. By the time you hit your stride, your reader may have wandered off.

Begin with something vivid or active. Sometimes, for dramatic purposes, your story should begin in what you think is the middle or even the end; try moving your beginnings, middles, and ends around. Cut and paste. (Not long ago writers had to do that with actual scissors and glue; what pleasure these computers be!) Remember, too, that as well as being dynamic, your start should give us a clue, a promise, about the direction of the whole piece.

There's nothing wrong with writing a runway to get your story moving. Sometimes you need a few lines or paragraphs or even pages to help figure out what you have in mind and where you're going. Write them. Get them down and give your story that first push.

But a few drafts later, when you know what your story is about, you might read the preparatory beginning and know it's not needed. Get rid of the runway.

Go back and check your stories. Are there places where you've sidled into a beginning? Would the piece be better starting somewhere else, with a bang? Try putting the middle at the start or the end, or the end at the beginning. It just might work.

The secret of having good ideas is to have a lot of ideas, then throw away the bad ones.

LINUS PAULING

Creativity is allowing yourself to make mistakes; art is knowing which ones to keep.

ANSEL ADAMS

At the start of any story, the narrative voice must take a firm grip on the reader and not let the reader's attention wander; the voice, in the beginning, is full of promises—bluffing, threatening, hints.

JOHN IRVING

19

Break your story into scenes

e

A student is reading an essay about growing up in Chicago with a crazy mother and an absent father; the writing is interesting and lively. But then she takes a deep breath and says the magic words: *One day* ... And we lean forward, because, until now, we've been listening to well-written generalities, set-up, and exposition. Now we are moving into a scene.

A scene occurs at a specific time and place with specific people, all clearly set up by the writer. It involves action, even if it's not physical but emotional action. A scene often involves dialogue. People talk and act; something happens, and we the readers are there. Good memoir writing means dramatizing, bringing to life. *One day* ...

In my years of teaching memoir and personal essay writing, I have heard many hundreds of essays. What I remember are the scenes. Here's an example: An Englishwoman, Mary, describing her childhood during the Blitz in 1941, wrote that though sugar was rationed, her mother once managed to get a box of chocolates. Mary illuminated the scene: five hungry children sitting at the table, each carefully picking one chocolate. Then Mother continued to pass the box until all the chocolates were gone, but Mary alone was not allowed to take another. She didn't write, *My mother loved her other children, but she did not love me.* She just showed the chocolate box sweeping by again and again, while her siblings chose and ate. That picture of the sometimes startling cruelty of parents has never left me. *One day, my mother brought home a box of chocolates ...*

And other scenes: a boy fondled sexually by his half-asleep father as they watched the hockey game *one night;* a little girl left *early one morning* in charge of her baby brother, which led to the boy's accidental drowning; *the day after 9/11,* a woman searching for her husband in a New York hospital; a stranger meeting a homeless child *one afternoon in Mexico City,* treating him to a hot meal and a clean, safe bed. These are burned into my brain.

Look at your list of the memorable stories you want to tell. Is it full of huge events or ones spanning long periods of time? The stories will be easier to tell and to read if you break them down into smaller pieces. Pick manageable events and anecdotes that contain scenes. Think small or you'll be overwhelmed.

Say you want to tell us about your wild, law-breaking adolescence. Instead of plunging into all seven or eight years, start with one summer or one week or one day or even one important hour, a microcosm that will bring those years into focus. Somewhere in the story, there will be an indelible scene. Paint it.

Imagine that Steven Spielberg calls you today and says, "You fascinating person, I want to make a movie of your life. Sketch out the ten life-changing scenes that must be in the film." Which scenes would they be? These are your vital stories, in scenes with context, conflict (with others, self, society), detail, dialogue. List them for Steve. Write them for us.

A reader doesn't want to hear what you have to say. A reader wants to hear a story you have to tell.

LEE GUTKIND

A story is a cohesive account of events in which something is at stake—a beginning, middle and end tied together with characters, scenes and details (long shots, mid shots, close-ups) that lead to a climax and resolution (or not).

IAN BROWN

20

Keep it to yourself—for now

ℰ

You've done it. You've found the place, the time, and the topic that thrills you, you've sat there long enough to throw lots into the giant handbag, and you've written a deliriously baggy first draft. You read it over and think it stinks, and then you rearrange, rewrite, ditch the runway, sharpen the scenes; you read it again and think, Is this possible? It sounds better. Even pretty good.

It's time, you think, for some feedback. You want someone else to read it.

Actually, you want someone to read it and tell you it's the best thing they've ever read. We all do.

So you turn to your life partner, your best friend, the co-worker in the next cubicle who likes the same kinds of books you do—anyone who will take the time to read your words and talk to you about them. My writing friends, please be careful about this. Non-writers who love you or work with you cannot be honest, objective judges of your writing ability. And why should they be? They might be threatened by the tone of your piece, or even by the very fact that you are setting off on this creative journey alone. Maybe your friends have a critical Mr. Ploux in their heads, too. You are just beginning, and they may judge you as they would judge Atwood or Ondaatje. You can get hurt.

Or else they may say that everything you write is brilliant, which feels good but is no help.

Be cautious to whom you show your work, particularly at the early stages. Vet your reviewers carefully, and be honest with yourself about what you want from them. Be aware that being edited, though necessary, can be a hurtful process. When you need perspective and don't have a teacher or friend whom you trust as an editor—or even better, an actual editor you trust as an editor—put the finished pages away in a drawer for a few days, or, even better, for weeks or perhaps months.

Hard though it probably will be, work on something else for a while. Then get the pages out again and read them carefully. To the best of your ability, read them imagining they were written by someone else; sometimes, to foster that illusion, I print the pages out in a font I don't ordinarily use. When you're more experienced, you could even imagine you're reading as one of your enemies. This will certainly give you a new and much clearer perspective.

**Until you are well on your way as a writer, exper-
ienced enough to take criticism and evaluate its use to
you—this is valuable, this is not—be careful about sharing
your work with anyone who is not an experienced and
empathetic editor or teacher or a trustworthy fellow
writer.** (See Step 44 on writers' groups.) Even your loved
ones. Particularly your loved ones.

Think of the voices and vocabulary you use in your
daily life: what stories you'd tell, and how, to a judge, a
childhood confidante, a teenaged son, a mother-in-law.
A different voice for each. When you write, you pick one
of those voices. There isn't one you, there's the narrative
voice you've chosen for this piece of work; for the next,
you may choose a funnier or more sarcastic or edgier
voice. You should be free to test voices without worrying
that someone may discover a side of you they don't know
and might not like. You might also be trying a new style,
or perhaps some of the stories themselves, ones you've
hidden and want to explore, may be too strange or dark for
your innocent readers.

So until you find an editor or writers' group you respect
and trust, keep this work to yourself. Test away.

Note: This step does not apply to Stephen King, whose
novelist wife Tabitha reads all his manuscripts. But then
Mr. King has made his own rules about almost everything,
and extremely successfully, too. (Suggestion—read his fine
book *On Writing: A Memoir of the Craft.*)

I have spent a good many years since—too many, I think—being ashamed about what I write. I think I was forty before I realized that almost every writer of fiction or poetry who has ever published a line has been accused by someone of wasting his or her God-given talent. If you write (or paint or dance or sculpt or sing, I suppose), someone will try to make you feel lousy about it, that's all.

STEPHEN KING

21

Claim your truth

I once wrote an essay about visiting my grandparents in their dark, stuffy apartment in New York. My father—allowed to read the piece late in the process—protested. "There was nothing dark and stuffy about that apartment!" he said. "In comparison with the others, it was flooded with sunlight." My childhood home in Halifax with its huge windows was the opposite of my grandparents' flat on West 79th with its dark shroud of curtains. But my dad grew up in places with fewer windows and heavier curtains.

It's your story, so you get to tell it your way. If my father had written the story, the apartment would have been bright.

I also believe you can, within sensible limits, change

slightly or "recreate" the truth in order to fashion a better tale. Two friends were with me when a fire broke out in my home, but in writing the story, I didn't need two by-standers to bring the drama to life, so I left one out. Her absence does not change the fundamental truth of the story: There was a fire and no one was hurt. Without an extra person, it's a cleaner, clearer tale. But that's as far as I would go with changes.

Beware of the pitfalls of fudging the facts. In 2006 James Frey's forced admission that his memoir *A Million Little Pieces* contained blatant exaggerations caused a huge controversy about the issue of truth in creative non-fiction. Frey originally wrote his book as fiction but was persuaded by his editors to call it a memoir. If they'd printed a brief disclaimer—"Parts of this story have been embellished for effect"—Oprah and a million readers would not have felt cheated.

There is no universal truth. Ask your siblings to describe a dinnertime or holiday ritual from your childhood; their memories and yours will be so different, you could have come from different families. In fact, you did. (See Mary's story in Step 19.) If they read your memoirs, they might be outraged. "It wasn't like that at all!" they might say. No, it wasn't, for them. But you are the one writing the story; your experiences and insights are unique. And you might also be reimagining the truth slightly to fashion a better story.

But only slightly. Beware of veering into fiction, a.k.a. making it all up, a.k.a. lying. And tell your siblings to write their own version.

After calling for honesty, I hope I don't bewilder you when I say writers can be too honest. *I don't remember exactly, but I think my mother worked in a circus when I was young* may be truthful, but it's also opaque. If you can't see the picture clearly, how will I? **Do not tell me what you don't remember** (unless the whole point of the story is that you don't remember). **Contact someone who does know or do other kinds of research.**

Without a way to ascertain something, you can make it up in the interests of a good story, but only to a certain point: only if it does not change the fundamental truth of your tale. If you have a general but not a specific memory of what you're writing, like dialogue between your parents when you were small, make it up. Those memories are buried in there somewhere. I'll bet what you write will be pretty close to what was actually said.

Be aware that this is controversial: Non-fiction writers who feel we should stay as close as possible to the strict letter of the truth will be outraged.

I preach there are all kinds of truth, your truth and somebody else's. But behind all of them there is only one truth and that is that there's no truth.

FLANNERY O'CONNOR

I have been corrected on some points, mostly of chronology. I've allowed some of these points to stand, because this is a book of memory, and memory has its own story to tell.

TOBIAS WOLFF

Si non e vero, e ben trovato. (Even if it's not true, it's a good story.)

VERDI

22

Unpack your suitcases

A student began to read her piece. *Excited about the prospect of going away to camp, I ran around getting my gear ready. As I searched for my sleeping bag, I wished that Mum hadn't left us and that she was there to help me. When the camp bus pulled up, I was first in line, eager for adventure …*

Wait a minute … what did you say? We're listening to a tale about going to camp and then suddenly there's a mother who has disappeared. Which is the more interesting story? Right there, in the middle of the paragraph, is a closed suitcase, a giant mystery waiting to be unpacked. We want to hear about Mum and won't be satisfied with zooming right by her off to camp.

The writer will have to unpack that suitcase right now, which means opening up the hugely important subject of a mother's disappearance and writing about it—if not in depth, because you don't want her to take over the camp story, then enough to explain. The reader needs to be enlightened and will fuss until you explain. Or else you had better leave your vanished and intriguing mother out of this story altogether. She probably deserves one of her own.

Sometimes we're so accustomed to lugging our suit-cases around that we don't even recognize them. This writer was so used to missing her mother, it was natural for her to bring up that loss when recalling her childhood. She didn't realize how curious we'd be about such a tantalizing subject. Often, in fact, the whole point of the essay or story *is* the suitcase; the writer has that topic pressing on mind and heart but, because it's so fraught, prefers to put it down, unopened, and rush on by. Perhaps secretly hoping that we'll notice it and ask. Perhaps not.

But if we're reading with any kind of attentiveness, we will notice. So you'd better have an explanation. (See Step 37.)

Good personal writing is about the process of dis-covery. The narrator is grappling with a problem, a pain, a life-changing moment, something that needs to be explored and understood before the journey can continue or end. That's why we read: to find out how the issue is resolved.

If you are busy hiding a key part of your story, you're not telling us the truth. And if you don't think enough of your readers to go deeply into the truth, why should we stay with you?

What are your suitcases? Are you trying to conceal them in the middle of your essays? Your readers are pointing at them and saying, "Open that! Now!"

Unpack.

When I start something and an instinct in me is saying don't go there, don't go there—that's where I know I have to go.

WAYSON CHOY

Your own winning literary style must begin with interesting ideas in your head. Find a subject you care about and which you in your heart feel others should care about. It is this genuine caring, and not your games with language, which will be the most compelling and seductive element of your style.

KURT VONNEGUT

PUT ON YOUR
EDITOR'S HAT

23

Paint the picture with details

ere is a perfectly good paragraph: *He drove me home fast in his old car. I felt really emotional when he told me what he'd be doing this summer and that he'd be around.*

Here's another paragraph: *As we sped home in his rusty grey Toyota, he told me he'd found a construction job. "I guess I'll be around this summer," he said. I gulped back tears.*

The two accomplish the same thing in terms of plot: drive home, conversation, emotion. The first just gets you there. The second paints a picture and draws you in. How? By using detail. Details paint pictures and bring a story to life.

Give the specifics. Don't generalize. Not *I opened a very big present wrapped in lurid colours* but *I could barely get my arms around the hot pink box with the orange bow.* Which can you see?

A memoirist once wrote that all he looked for was one small sensory detail from his past. He'd hang onto that—the smell of boiled cabbage, the sound of high heels clicking on the stairs—and use it, like a thread, to guide him further into the story. That's how exploration of memory works. When the thread of your own recollections won't take you very far, however, you can supplement them with research, which will give you great details even if they're not exactly yours. Be careful not to go too far, as I pointed out in Step 21. But in some instances, who will know?

As Dad made lunch, he sadly remembered his piloting experiences toward the end of World War II.

Dad wept on the grilled cheese sandwiches as he told us of his months in 1944 piloting B-52s over Japan.

Which can you see? Sensory details pull us in and bring the story to life.

Write about your favourite room in your house while sitting in another room. Write about the first bedroom, the first schoolroom you can remember. See how much detail comes back to you. Work at it; for some of us, without easy access to early memory, remembering is hard. Close your eyes and focus; try to see one small part of the picture in your mind, then widen the lens.

Learn the names of things; trees, flowers, and birds have specific names. Don't just say you're reading a book or listening to music; give me the title. **Paint the picture with details.** But not too much detail. Give us enough colour that we see vividly, but not so much that your story submerges us and grinds to a halt.

If you find yourself having trouble getting into a story you want to tell, it is always a good idea to get up very close and start using your senses ... These acts of memory ... push your story deeper, pull your reader closer, and lift the heart of the story out of obscurity into a sensory world that you and your readers can inhabit together.

JUDITH BARRINGTON

The writer should never be ashamed of staring. There is nothing that does not require his attention.

FLANNERY O'CONNOR

24

Develop your ear
for dialogue

Here is a perfectly good sentence: *She told me she was very angry at me.*

Here is another sentence: *"I hate your stupid face, scumbag!" she said.*

Dialogue is a powerful tool. When you let us hear your characters in conversation, we're there in the room with them. Writing dialogue is a kind of playwriting. You need to be aware of each character's unique rhythm, vocabulary, and slang—including your own. How quickly you bring us into a teenager's room by reporting what is being said: *"Like, eleven, that is so whack, man, you suck epically."* Rather than *My sixteen-year old expressed his displeasure at my imposition of a curfew.* (And incidentally, that adolescent dialogue will soon be dated and will need to be rewritten regularly.)

Eavesdrop. Pay attention to how people express themselves. Those of you who take extended rides on public transit have been given a gift—so many voices chatting as if in a private room (yay cell phones!). Take note and even surreptitiously jot down turns of phrase and idiosyncrasies of language. Character is rhythm; if you catch the rhythm of a person's sentences, you'll be able to bring him or her to life. Later, read what you've written aloud to yourself and listen carefully for cadence and vocabulary, to make sure it sounds authentic.

Read like a writer; learn how others use dialogue. Some novels by the Irish master Roddy Doyle consist almost entirely of characters in conversation: We're sitting in a Dublin pub, engulfed in cigarette smoke, part of the scene. (Suggestion—read Doyle and J.D. Salinger for their brilliant dialogue.)

An important technical note: Your characters don't need to warble or counter or query or muse. Most of the time, a simple "said" or "asked" is enough. Rather than having your heroine giggle, bluster, or screech, let me hear how she says it by what she says. And please leave out small talk—"Hi, how are you?" "Fine, thanks, how are you?"—unless the point is that your characters have nothing interesting to say. Distill dialogue to its essence.

What things do your loved ones say that define them? What expressions make you laugh or cringe? Write them down. My brilliant Uncle Edgar, a champion bridge player, was so articulate, I knew that, when I wrote about him, I'd never be able to remember or reinvent the way he spoke. So when we talked on the phone, I took notes. At his memorial, I was able to tell the mourners that once, during his illness, I asked, "How are you?" A normal person might have said, "Tired." But Uncle Edgar said, "I am prey to lassitude. I'm in no distress, but vigour is almost totally absent." Does this give you a clue to his character? That's the point.

Try to tell a story using only dialogue, to establish and situate your characters with their own unique voices and enhance the story.

If you are writing dialogue—say it aloud as you write it. Only then will it have the sound of speech.

JOHN STEINBECK

Writing dialogue is a gift and a craft. You can learn how to do it. Dialogue must read as essential poetry. Every word counts and moves the narrative forward. If you have to say how or why the dialogue was said, redo it. It should integrate and carry the information. Real-life dialogue has no place in literature; it should be heightened reality.

WAYSON CHOY

25

Beware of w*r*i*t*i*n*g* and jargon

The aforementioned Uncle Edgar was a witty, erudite writer. I once showed him an essay I'd written which included the line, "She had myriad aches and pains." I expected him to compliment me on my sophisticated vocabulary, written in imitation of his. Instead, he asked, "Why are you using a five-dollar word like 'myriad'? What's wrong with 'a lot of'? 'Many'? In writing, always use fifty-cent words when you can. Be sparing with those fancy expensive ones."

To paraphrase: Keep your prose simple. Make it clear. Almost all great writers use fifty-cent words precisely, with a rich five-dollar beauty thrown in when needed.

Some beginning writers like to use an ornate style I

call W*R*I*T*I*N*G*. They will bring in an essay that's a cornucopia (there's a good expensive one) of five-dollar words. The work is not about sharing an insight or experience, it's a thesaurus on parade. Sentences groan under the weight of unwieldy or poetic words and phrases, behind which it's difficult to catch that important goal of the writing process: meaning.

This ornate fog can afflict famous writers, too, especially poets who turn to prose. Their use of language may be dazzling, but what in the book is happening to whom? We're lost in a thicket of poesy.

Attaining simplicity and clarity is also difficult for academics and technical writers, who are not just encouraged but obligated to use impenetrable jargon. A young friend who teaches university economics asked me to vet an essay. It was written in convoluted "economese" incomprehensible to an outsider, and I suggested she translate it into clear, readable English. "My colleagues won't take me seriously if I don't use language their way," she replied, and left her article as it was, for her peers only.

Yes, technical jargon is a shorthand for insiders, which is to say it also keeps everyone else out. The education system is one of the worst offenders; when I received flyers from my children's school, I'd try to translate them from educationese into English. Not to mention lawyers and their impenetrable, expensive legalese.

One of your jobs, even if you're not a poet, is to find exactly the right word. If you can't find it, use a thesaurus or a dictionary to hunt it down. Those resources are part of your tool chest, too. But don't let the choice overwhelm you. Better one exactly right word than three nearlys.

Look at the writing you've done. Are there unnecessarily complex or fancy words? Any jargon? Can you exchange expensive words for the invaluable two-bit workhorses of language?

He that uses many words for explaining any subject doth, like the cuttlefish, hide himself for the most part in his own ink.

JOHN RAY

I pushed too hard at the ideas. When you're young, you're writing for your life. You tend to be grandiose. Eventually, I learned to relax.

FRANK KERMODE

All young poets wear poetry sunglasses. I took off the goggles, and then I could let in humour, personality, all the things I was excluding. The main thing was simplifying my vocabulary. Eventually, I was confident enough to write a simple sentence, and then I began to recognise the sound of my own writing.

BILLY COLLINS

26

Be sparing with adverbs, adjectives, similes, and metaphors

There's a well-known story about a writer who brought his editor a six-hundred-page manuscript. When he got it back, it had been cut in half.

"What the hell have you done to my work?" he asked.

"I cut the adjectives and adverbs," the editor replied.

An adverb is a word that modifies the verb, the action word. Adverbs are often unnecessary; they litter your sentences like discarded candy wrappers marring a forest trail. *He grinned gleefully at me,* or, *"You're breaking my heart," I cried sadly.* Sometimes there's a string of adverbs in the same sentence: *Suspiciously and angrily but slowly, she walked to the door.*

A rule: The adverb is not needed when the verb is

doing its job. Grinning is usually gleeful; crying is usually sad. You need the adverb only if the verb needs modification for clarity: *He grinned malevolently at me.* Better, though, to search for a verb that incorporates the qualities carried by the adverb: *He leered at me.*

Excessive use of adverbs shows that a W*R*I*T*E*R* is at work, someone who'd rather muddy the line with excess verbiage than make sure it's transparent. Yet students look at me as if I'm murdering fine art when I suggest slashing their adverbs. There are times, yes, when an adverb is necessary; just choose them carefully and use them sparingly. There—that was just one of those times: "Carefully" and "sparingly" are needed for clarity.

The same goes for adjectives—descriptive words. Don't tell me the garden is lush, overgrown, and luxuriant, three words that mean almost the same thing; find the right word. An occasional cloudburst of adjectives is allowed, but don't drown us with them. Eventually we'll suffer from sensory overload and stop seeing anything at all. (Suggestion—read *Cider with Rosie* by Laurie Lee, the king of sensory overload, and see how he gets away with it. Or not.)

Be sparing with metaphors—*cloudburst of adjectives* is a metaphor—and similes, phrases that employ "like" or "as"—*like discarded candy wrappers.* Used judiciously (an adverb), like a strong spice (simile), they add enormously (adverb) to the colours of your piece (metaphor). Used indiscriminately (adverb), they bury us in comparisons and poetics.

It is virtually guaranteed that an editor will cut your piece, and you may not like the results. Better learn to do it for yourself first. **Here is one of the most important exercises of all: Take a piece you have written recently and cut it in half. If it's a thousand words long, chop until it's five hundred.**

Of course something will be lost, perhaps something important, as well as flights of rhetorical fancy and a lot of adjectives and adverbs. But when you are forced to inspect and justify every word, something more important will be gained: Your piece will emerge in its uncluttered beauty. Its beautiful bones will show.

Writers who have nothing to say always strain for metaphors to say it in.

FLORENCE KING

Like Toni Morrison, Elmore Leonard has a particular dislike for adverbs. "I would never use a word like quietly," he says. "There's a pause with the ly that stops everything. I'll say, 'He used a quiet voice.'"

BEN YAGODA

27

Avoid clichés and wishy-washy definers

❧

Like abstract words—truth, beauty—that are vague and elusive, a cliché will cloud your stories. I call clichés "oil slick words," because when readers come to them, they skid right over. Clichéd expressions have been used so often, we don't know what they mean any more, and we don't care. Black as coal, right as rain, sparkling like diamonds, like a pig in clover. Do you see any pictures? I bet you slid right on by.

Clichés were once original. One January long ago, a minstrel sitting near a window cried, "Egad, yonder shirt is of a whiteness much like … snow!" And everyone thought, "What poetic cleverness is this. Methinks I too will compare white things to snow." By the millionth time something white was compared to snow, we weren't listening.

So any time an expression slides too easily from your pen—soft as a baby's cheek, live and learn, tired but happy—check to make sure it's not an oil slick cliché. There are sites on the Internet that list them, so you can check. When in doubt, find a fresh way, your own original way, to say it.

Also to avoid, unless absolutely necessary, are wishy-washy modifiers: perhaps, sort of, rather, a bit. If you dilute your story—*I kind of thought I was making a mistake*—your reader will get lost. "Probably" makes the picture fuzzy. Paint with bold, clear lines. Make your prose vivid, not vague; vigorous, not vapid. (And beware of cute, self-conscious tricks like using the same letter over and over, a.k.a. alliteration.)

Go through your work and check for clichés and wishy-washy words. Pounce on maybe, almost, soft as a dove, fits like a glove. **Make your sentences definite and original.**

For inspiration, talk to a very small child about an imaginary world. Get right down on the floor and invent something together. Nothing hesitant, apologetic, judgemental, or clichéd about that imagination.

Last, but not least, avoid clichés like the plague.

WILLIAM SAFIRE

28

Leave messages
to Western Union

When Hollywood producer Sam Goldwyn encountered writers who had a message to impart, he urged them simply to send a telegram. "Pictures," he said, "are for entertainment."

During our first class, when I ask the participants to tell us why they've come to writing school and what they hope to gain, often someone will say, "I want to tell my story because I've learned a lot about life, and I'd like to help others by telling what I know. I think I can make a difference."

These are noble, generous sentiments; they're just not often a solid starting place for truthful memoir or personal essay writing. If you want to write an inspirational or how-to book about, say, body image, please do so, but not in the guise of a memoir. To share your experience of learning to love your body, don't hand me your message; show me your story. Take me into the life of a miserable, overweight or anorexic young girl; paint the picture clearly and vividly and show me, with detail, dialogue, and all the other tools in your kit, how she came to love herself. That way I will walk into the tale and come to know its heroes and villains but will be free to draw my own conclusions. Maybe I'll learn something different, even something more than you'd imagined.

In a memoir, please do not tell me what to think. **Don't point out your conclusions. Do not judge the characters, the situation, even—no, especially—yourself.** Lead me into the story, create vivid scenes, breathe the characters to life, and let me figure things out for myself. Try not to lecture, diagnose, or preach; trust the reader to understand.

Beware vague, abstract words, however much you love them and use them in speech: shame, trust, forgiveness. Instead, show me concrete things—a tempting chocolate bar, an estranged friend's hug—and what they mean to you. Enchant me and draw me in. I'll gladly go with you.

Some students feel self-indulgent taking the time to write down their stories. They justify the effort by telling themselves they're not doing it for selfish reasons but for others. Exploring your own experiences, memories, and thoughts is important work. No need to rationalize it by turning it into a sermon.

I'd rather see a sermon
than hear one any day;
I'd rather one should walk with me
than merely tell the way.

EDGAR GUEST

Make your scenes resonate with life, not with
conclusions. Do not write about social injustice.
It's more exciting to write about how it feels to be
a victim of social injustice, so the reader feels it
too and is moved to make change.

WAYSON CHOY

29

Pace your writing

Survey your work on the page. Sometimes just the look can reveal what might be problematic. Are all your sentences the same length? Are your paragraphs so long that each page is a solid block of print?

Short pause.

New paragraphs provide breaks and space so the reader can take a breath. Readers also need variety in sentence structure and length, or the monotony of your rhythm, no matter how fascinating your subject, will put them to sleep.

Always read your work out loud and listen for tempo and pace. Vary the length and structure of your sentences and paragraphs.

Take those writers who say "Join me," and type or write out five pages of their work. Analyse them as painters check brushstrokes. Deconstruct. Highlight short, medium, long sentences in different colours. Check for rhythm, pacing, length. Do the same with a boring book, and find out why it's boring. Readers are kept awake by sleight of hand.

WAYSON CHOY

30

Show, don't tell

The clichéd image of a writing class is a teacher intoning "Show, don't tell." But what does that mean, exactly? "Showing" means the narrator is in the thick of the action at ground level, bringing to life what we see, hear, and learn, rather than simply reporting. It means dramatizing rather than recounting. When you report on rather than animate a scene, you are telling. When you deliver a message in your piece (*I learned that* ...), you are telling.

Telling is reportage. Creative writing is "recreating": illuminating your tale from within with detail, dialogue, scenes ...

• *I found the whole idea of school frightening and didn't want my mother to leave me there. The tall nuns*

*scared me, and so did the loud noise made by the many
other children.*

•   *Hot tears scalded my cheeks. I clung to my mother's
hand, heart thudding, stomach heaving at the sight of
giant women like crows in long black gowns, and the
hordes of children, shrieking.*

Which passage invites you in to the experience, illumi-
nates it, and brings it to life? Which is telling from a distance
and which is showing the moment? In the second, you
feel the camera zooming in to establish the action and setting, or the binoculars enlarging the picture to present the
details. We, too, can hear, see, and, most importantly, feel.

Some telling is necessary in almost every piece, because
exposition is needed to situate us. Only a play or screen-
play is entirely showing, with no intrusion of the author's
voice for explanation or enlightenment. The key for most
personal essays and memoir is balance: scenes, drama, and
dialogue balanced with exposition and narration to help a
piece not just make sense but take flight.

**Think of an incident that happened to you yester-
day. Write about it as a reporter, listing time, character,
and event:** *And then, I ...* **Now go back; begin, line by line,
to show rather than tell about the experience.** Zoom in;
open up all your senses. Use your tool kit: detail, dialogue, descriptives, suspense, pace, rhythm. Get inside the
moment and crack it open. That's how unforgettable stories
are told.

Go back and look again at your past writing. Are there
places where you're standing apart and simply recounting?

Places where you can you go into the heart of the event and recreate it in all its colourful and emotional detail?

Important note: The rules are different for traditional expository essays like those by the great Michel de Montaigne, who, more than three hundred years ago, asked himself "What do I know?" and proceeded to find out by writing the first "essaies": "Of Age," "Of Drunkenness," "Of Thumbs," and many more. Or those of John McPhee, a *New Yorker* writer who delves into topics as diverse as the atomic bomb, geology, Russian art, fishing, and oranges. "The essay," said Aldous Huxley, "is a literary device for saying almost everything about almost anything." As well as presenting objective facts, these essays explore point of view and authorial voice rather than storyline and are not dramatized like personal essays. They typically involve more telling than showing.

Suggestion: Try writing an expository essay about a topic that fascinates you. Do some research. Explore your own thought process. Investigate. The story is about you discovering something and enlightening us about the journey. Start with "Of ..." or "On ..."

In creative non-fiction, the writer recreates the experience, recreates how he came to a certain

insight, in order to draw the reader in, not to teach.

WAYSON CHOY

Don't tell me the moon is shining; show me the glint of light on broken glass.

ANTON CHEKHOV

31

Try out your light voice

To misquote the actress: "Make 'em smile and they'll like you, they'll really like you."

I used to ask my students to try writing something humorous. Humour is a gift, I said. Making people smile is a way of building a bridge to them, extending a friendly hand. God knows we all need to laugh.

But writing humorously is difficult, much more difficult than simply being an amusing person. How few really funny personal essay writers there are: in the past, Stephen Leacock, Mark Twain, E.B. White, Erma Bombeck, and more recently Dave Barry, David Sedaris, Nora Ephron, Toronto's Marni Jackson. Writing with humour is more than a skill, it's a calling, and it's definitely a frightening challenge for those to whom it does not come naturally.

So I now talk in my classes not about humour but about finding and using "the light voice." A light voice can sound detached or bemused and can tell a story in a quirky, informal way—not trying to make people laugh, simply choosing a tone that is bright rather than heavy. A light voice does not mean lack of depth, just a buoyancy of attitude. It's still a gift, still a hand reaching out to greet.

The best way to try out your light voice is to pick the right story. When you've had a bit to drink and are sitting comfortably with family or friends, what are the tales you like to tell? Usually there's a humiliating anecdote about yourself that's amusing now, though it wasn't at the time. To lighten a story, you can exaggerate the haplessness of the narrator and star—you. Bump up your personality. Some comic writers, like Dave Barry, overstate, making extreme exaggeration their trademark. Others, like Woody Allen, make wry understatement the focus of their comedy. Some are cynical, some flippant or goofy, some brutally frank to the point of shock.

Read your favourite funny men and women first as a reader, to laugh, and then as a writer, to analyse what techniques they use to tickle you: exaggeration, understatement, absurdity, incongruity, irony, contrast, the outrageous, misunderstanding, innuendo, word plays, put-downs ...

Writers often use the light voice to highlight the hilarious foibles of their significant others, who may not be happy to see their craziest deeds in print. David Sedaris writes with scary candidness and wit not just about himself but about his parents, siblings, and lovers. We the readers are grateful, but sometimes—he tells us so himself—his loved ones are not. How far you go to make us smile is up to you. (See Step 40 on discretion.)

On my website under Podcasts is one of my attempts at the light voice, "The Cheese Tray." The event was embarrassing then. I hope it's funnier now.

Give it a try. Think of an amusing story, relax, amplify your voice, and invite us to enjoy the oddball nature of the experience with you.

Tragedy plus time equals comedy.

STEVE ALLEN

Lightness does not mean without depth. A writer like Erma Bombeck gives us lightness with depth. Orchestrate the natural comedic tone, from which will come the depth.

WAYSON CHOY

I hate reality but it's still the best place to get a good steak.

WOODY ALLEN

I love being a writer. What I can't stand is the paperwork.

PETER DE VRIES

32

Don't be nice

Even when you use humour to show it, drama is crisis. Without crisis, without conflict and dilemma, a narrative risks being flat and uninteresting. We'll drift away. Yet some writers, especially we women, prefer to avoid problems and crisis. We don't want to make a fuss in our writing, draw attention to ourselves. And God forbid we should show a side or use a voice that is angry or outraged. Because we have been trained to be nice.

Nice is boring.

How many good writers are just nice and nothing else— not sharp-eyed or satirical or deadly honest? Name one. "The cradle rocks above an abyss," writes Vladimir Nabokov in his seminal memoir *Speak, Memory* (suggestion—

read it). Not a pretty image, but true. Life is not nice, and neither are the creatures who populate it. Even our saints and heroes have an ugly, interesting side. Showing only the sweet stuff is dishonest and, frankly, dull. What is popular reality television about? Watching others go through stressful, humiliating, or dangerous situations. We crave compelling drama. Nice does not cut it.

Find the places in your work where you said to yourself, "That's not very nice—I don't think I'll write that." Where you censored yourself and changed a violent emotion to a more acceptable one. Now write the true feeling in all its dangerous glory. That's the interesting you, the complex person, the writer with all kinds of internal colours, not just sunshine yellow and baby blue— but pitch black, bruise purple, and slime green, too. Paint them. Then you'll be real. Your readers will connect to and remember not your perfection but your humanity.

Again, make sure your sentences are active rather than passive. Writers hoping to avoid both painting an ugly picture and deploying the "I" word write sentences dense with passive constructions: *The pot was thrown in anger at the wall.* We see nothing except a flying pot. Who threw it? Your sentences should have an active subject— someone doing something. You're furious. Throw the goddamn pot!

Go back and check your work. Can you find sentences where nobody does anything? Make sure each has a subject—a doer. And make sure they're doing something that matters, even if it's unpleasant.

He who dares not offend cannot be honest.

THOMAS PAINE

To me, finding voice is about confidence. Typically, when your mother starts to dislike your writing, that's when you've really found your voice. You've come to an honesty that's maybe causing some discomfort to the people around you, as opposed to writing pretty in an entertaining libretto way.

ABRAHAM VERGESE

33

Build to a moment
of change or reflection

What separates a piece of non-fiction as literature, like a personal essay, from a diary entry? The tone can be the same, say, chatty and confidential, or spare and direct, but the shape is not. A piece of literature is sculpted to lead somewhere: to grab the reader, unfurl the story, and then, at some point, to reveal why the story is being told. A crafted piece leads somehow, somewhere, to struggle, realization, decision, illumination, transformation.

We read to go on a voyage of discovery with the author—to connect, be amazed, find out what happens next, even be shown something new. For your work to thrill us, something has to happen. We begin somewhere with you, hoping either to end somewhere else, or to find ourselves back in the same place but somehow different. Changed.

To be effective and grab the reader, most pieces of personal writing lead to at least one moment of clarity, reflection, or change.

We talked in Step 19 about the scene; often, but not always, the vital moment comes in an important scene. The change or reflection does not have to be earth-shattering; it can be minuscule or can seem so until you look more closely. It can be a split-second moment or a very long episode or anything in between. But it should be there. Otherwise, the reader does not know why you are telling this particular story. When you reveal the moment of clarity or change, then I understand: Ahhh, this is why. This is the dramatic moment in which I enter the story fully, put myself in the place of the writer, and grasp what he or she is going through and showing me.

This is the moment when you will connect most strongly with your audience. It can be in the first line, the last line, or anywhere in between. But it needs to be there.

Please make sure this intense moment comes, not in a message delivered to us by the narrator but out of the action of the story. Remember, we don't want a lesson. We want to be shown the reason, in a moment of transformation, that we've embarked on this excursion with you.

Review the stories you want to tell and the ones you have told. Make sure you have found, for each, the moment of change or insight.

Here are a few examples of moments of change, from my own work and that of my students.

- *As I stood watching my friend tuck in her baby, a force so strong punched into my chest that I gasped for breath and nearly fell backward against the doorframe. One thought overpowered me: a child. I must have my own child.*

- *It was in Mr. Smith's Standard One class that I first broke the rules. It was show and tell. "When I grow up, I'm going to spit on God," I announced.*

- *It's time to write about Barbara. The thought hit me as if winging through the frost-covered window, a clear voice ordering me to dig out Barbara's letters, see what was there.*

- *"Get in the car," he said, and so began the ride that changed my life.*

- *On the island of Crete one day, I heard of a group about to make the gruelling trek down the Samaria Gorge. What was suddenly different that day? I don't know. It just was. This time I didn't want to miss out on adventure. Yes, I said.*

- *"Positive"—famous last word of my old life, first of a new one.*

In your reading, watch for the moments of insight, reflection, and change. Often they're vivid and unforgettable—which is the whole point.

How sharp a rent a handful of moments made in the fabric of a life.

GUY GAVRIEL KAY

If nothing happens, it's not a story.

FLANNERY O'CONNOR

[Students] may not make their self-discoveries during the time they work with me, but it is my business to spot the revelatory moments in their writing, and to pause and say, "Here you are." When I find something essential in their work, I am helping them get a glimpse of themselves.

ROGER ROSENBLATT

34

Check your work for bows

There are those of us—we teachers are in the forefront of this group—who believe that without help and repetition, the poor reader won't grasp what we want to say. They need a clue, we think—a great big hint at the end, a final repeat of the message. So we finish by going over again what we have spent the whole piece showing.

My daughter smiled. "You know, Mum, you may actually be right," she said. She leaned over to kiss me, and, after months of combat, we hugged. I realized that mothers and daughters will always have difficulty finding the balance of power, but that the effort is truly worth the struggle.

Aww, that's sweet. It's also cloying and redundant. That last sentence repeats the entire essay. Try reading the above out loud with and without the last sentence. I call the last little bit the bow; the writer is wrapping things up with a shiny satin message, a final flourish of illumination for the reader to cherish. But if the piece is written well enough, the readers will draw their own conclusions without a last helpful homily.

Cut it.

Leave them wanting more. A slightly ambiguous ending haunts us, forcing us to think back. Trust the intelligence of your readers; they can figure it out and will resent being force-fed a tidy conclusion.

Usually you should begin your story as far into the action as you can, and you should end your story as expeditiously as you can. Don't drag it out. Finish before you've made everything explicit. If the writing is good, the reader will fill in the rest.

Even if you love your dragged-out ending, cut it, unless your essay is incomprehensible without it, in which case you need to go back and look at the whole piece again. If you've done a good job, the reader will get what you want to say.

See? I just did it. Those last five lines are a useless, repetitive bow. If I weren't making a point about bows, I would have cut them.

Check your work for bows. The impulse behind them is generous and concerned: You just want to be sure they get it. Trust your readers. Trust your words.

It is with words as with sunbeams—the more they are condensed, the deeper they burn.

ROBERT SOUTHEY

35

Rewrite, rewrite, rewrite

I once asked a talented student if she'd done some work on a good story that we'd suggested she revise.

"Oh no, I never revise," she said. "I love writing. I hate rewriting."

"Then you're in the wrong class," I said.

Beginners don't realize that writing always means rewriting. Always. Literature is an art form in which a critic—the editor—is built right into the process. Writers reach a point when, immersed in their material, they cannot step back and see clearly what's on the page; they need skilled help to do so. No art editor stood in the studio telling Picasso to redo his painting because he'd used too much blue (though painters do comment this way for each other). But every writer of any worth has had some painstaking professional say, "This doesn't work, this is too long, this part is in the wrong place." All published writers have been edited.

As we learned in Step 14, your job as a writer is first to get a lot of stuff onto the page. Then you go over and over it, seeing how to make it better. Does it start and end in the right place? Can it be clearer? What about tense, grammar, punctuation? Can you find more effective words? Do you go deeply enough into the story? Is there a moment of change?

And in the final drafts, what can be cut? Every word should belong. Cutting is one of the most important jobs for any writer. You can do it yourself or wait for your editor to take out those long, sharp scissors. **Ask yourself what you can take out while still maintaining the integrity of the piece.**

At first, you'll be protective of your words. As you gain experience, you will learn that, if a hunch is making you look twice at a word, a page, or even a chapter, it probably isn't needed. "Kill your darlings" is a famous and often helpful instruction to writers; sometimes you should cut the very words and sentences you love the most. Cut them and save them in a file. They haven't disappeared. They're just not cluttering up your current piece. See how much better it is without them? And if it's not, put them back.

To repeat the "cutting in half" exercise of Step 26: In the editing stage, your job is to take out the big unnecessary things and then start on the small. To cut every single word that is not needed, including "the" and "and." (One example of the small: the word "that." *I knew that ... She'd decided that ...* Often, "that" can be removed, making the sentence cleaner.)

Remember one of the most important rules of writing: What you take out of your work is just as important as what you leave in.

This goes not only for words but also for incidents and scenes. You are writing about your life, and you've had quite a life. So when you sit to put scenes on paper, a great many come crowding in. This is a profoundly different process from writing fiction, where writers invent whole worlds and their characters, drawing them from their imagination. Memoirists choose which, of the millions of stories that have made up their lives so far, will work for a reader and advance their narrative. Not inventing, but selecting and sculpting.

So again, for a creative non-fiction writer, the decision about the scenes to leave out is as important as the choice of those to put in. In your first draft, include all those tales, yes. But in subsequent drafts, determine what your story is really about and take out any scene that's not needed to advance the action.

Put them in a file to use somewhere else, but do take them out. Our lives are cluttered and full, but that does not mean our stories have to be.

It's hard to edit your own work. Sometimes you cannot see what the problem is or even if there is one. Time and distance help. I once wrote an essay with a first line

I thought was moving and resonant—perfect. But the piece would not work, no matter how I pushed, pulled, and rewrote. So I put the pages away for months. When I got them out again, it was instantly clear to me that the problem was the first line; it set up the wrong direction for the entire piece. I cut the line and rewrote the beginning, and the whole essay suddenly made sense.

When you think a piece is finished, put it away for a while. When you reread it, you'll see more clearly that it's probably not.

I think of the work as six, six, and six. Six drafts to get the ideas onto the paper; six drafts to figure out what the piece is actually about, what the spine is; and six drafts to take out everything that doesn't fit once I know where the piece is going.

WAYSON CHOY

The pleasure IS the rewriting.

JOYCE CAROL OATES

36

Review the rules
of grammar

ご

Advanced students protest that I'm being impossibly
picky when I focus on points of grammar in critiqu-
ing their work. We don't go much into grammar in the early
stages; it's important just to get started. But if they wish to
be published, I tell them, correct grammar and punctuation
are essential.

We read, for example, *Running and skipping into the
house, my grandmother welcomed me with a hug.* Can
you see what's wrong?

"My, your granny was energetic," I say, pointing out
the misplaced modifier that makes the sentence read as
if the grandmother is running. Misplaced modifiers are

a common grammatical error; I see them all the time in newspapers.

"But it's clear the sentence means I'm the one running, not her, if you read it again," the student says.

"But you don't want readers to have to read it again," I reply.

Each time a careless bit of writing snags readers' attention from the story, each time they have to stop to make sense of something, you've lost them. Your readers want to be engrossed in your world, not jerked out of it and reminded that they're reading.

"Snags" is the term I use for points in a manuscript where a reader is pulled from the story by sloppy writing. When even a minor, common grammatical issue—a misplaced comma, a confusing tense switch—snags your readers, their journey with you has been interrupted. If they stop reading once too often, they may not start again.

There are great books and websites about grammar and punctuation, like the classic *Elements of Style* by Strunk and White, *Eats, Shoots and Leaves* by Lynne Truss, and thegrammarlady.com. (There's a partial list at the end of the book.) Don't worry about grammatical details when you're just beginning; you don't want to stop the flow by fiddling with participles and colons. But later, if you want your words to move out into the world, you'll have to.

Don't rely on an automatic computer program to do the correcting for you. Often, they're more confused than we are.

When you put on your editor's hat to rewrite, begin by clarifying what the story is about. Then pick out the snags, one by one, and replace them with clear constructions that never jolt the reader.

The most common mistake my students make is punctuation in quotations. So here are examples of the way dialogue punctuation should look.

> *I said, "Please come."*
>
> *"Please come," I said.*
>
> *"Don't come," I said. "It will upset Mother."*
>
> *"Please," I said, "don't upset our mother."*
>
> *"Are you coming?" I asked.*
>
> *"Are you coming," I asked, "or are you going to stay?"*
>
> *"Go away!" I shouted.*

Each time a new person speaks, begin a new paragraph. This helps readers follow the dialogue—it clarifies who is speaking—so you don't have to put "Suzie said," "I said," every time.

As I've already said, "said" is a good verb. Use it a lot. Use the others—burbled, muttered, chanted, snarled, growled—sparingly.

And ...

Always check your work for tense switches. It's easy to start in the present tense—*It's 1978 and I'm in the back seat of my parents' Chevrolet*—and then switch to the past —*My mother turned and shouted, "I don't want to hear another word!"* And then back again—*The silence in the car is louder than any argument.*

We've all done it without noticing. For readers, however, it's a big snag.

I believe a story can be wrecked by a faulty rhythm in a sentence—especially if it occurs toward the end—or a mistake in paragraphing, even punctuation. Henry James is the maestro of the semicolon. Hemingway is a first-rate paragrapher. From the point of view of ear, Virginia Woolf never wrote a bad sentence. I don't mean to imply that I successfully practice what I preach. I try, that's all.

TRUMAN CAPOTE

DIG DOWN

37

Open the doors
to the dark and deep

Much personal writing stems from, and deals with, hurt. After hearing hundreds of stories, I know that the one constant in human experience is the pain of being alive, particularly during childhood. An attractive but stiff forty-something student once asked the class, "Why are you people telling all these depressing, ghoulish stories? Why can't you just be cheerful?" She'd had a happy childhood and was happily married, she said; the only negative event of her life was a hurricane. In my many years of teaching, she is the only student who had no pain to report. Or none, perhaps, that she chose to remember.

Of course a writer does not need to have had an unhappy childhood in order to create successfully. But I will say this: It helps. That is, it helps if the childhood was unhappy enough, and usually lonely enough, to breed a thoughtful, compassionate adult, but not so terrible that a young soul was permanently damaged or even destroyed. The child who, for one reason or another, feels isolated and alone often spends time reading and pondering and grows up to be an adult who watches, who tries to figure out motivations, who knows how to be solitary. In other words, a potential writer.

Mind you, lots of great writers had happy childhoods. Fret not, you unfortunates who did. The happily neurotic E.B. White salutes you.

Why bother to write about the bad things that have happened to us, in childhood or later? Why not, as my student said, leave the dark side alone and focus on the sunny? Because all of us have encountered difficulty as well as joy, and we need to tell the truth. Concealing important stories because they happen to be painful is exhausting, often more tiring than simply bringing them out into the open. I am a great believer in opening the basement doors, behind which stories fester in silence. Not as therapy, though I do think revealing a hard or frightening truth to a considerate listener can be therapeutic. But because opening them frees you both as a person and as a writer. Too much energy and effort go into keeping them closed.

Open the doors and let the secrets fly out, so you can get on with all the other stories you have to tell. More students than I'd have believed possible have decided in class to tell tales of physical, emotional, or sexual abuse, often for the first time. A few do it as therapy, yes, and once the tale is told, they feel no need to write anything else. But most do it to liberate themselves from one soul-devouring story that is blocking the others. Let it out, get it down, read it, and weep. And then move on.

When people hear about my classes, even when they're in them, they opine that I'm "doing therapy," as if this is something bad. I used to reply, "I'm not interested in therapy but in good writing, which means exploring all of a writer's most important stories, happy but also sad ..."

Now I'm less defensive. What's wrong with therapy, for God's sake? We can all use a little, and some of us can use a lot. I'm not a therapist, but I am there to help writers pry open concealed doors, closed against truths and stories. There's no question that acknowledging a wound or a seminal event, putting it down on paper, and having it validated by others is a therapeutic endeavour. Well, hooray.

Such writing might never go out into the world. But getting it on paper will almost certainly free all the other stories and make the writer bigger, deeper, and braver.

I have, on occasion, taught talented students with giant blind spots in their lives, writers who cannot write truthfully because they cannot bear to see the truth. I have actually said, "I think a good therapist will help you as a writer."

I'm lucky to have had a lot of valuable therapy myself. But I don't write about it much. Beware of bringing your actual therapeutic experiences into your writing; they get dull quickly—like telling people your dreams, which I also think you should avoid. Don't go on about your wonderful therapist unless her work with you is the whole and only point. We can't all have your therapist, so we'd rather see you work things out for yourself.

I also strongly suggest, as in Step 28, that you do not set yourself up in your work as a judge. Often, writers will stand back from the story and hurl blame—at others, or more destructively, at themselves. *What an idiot—how could I not have seen what a liar she was?* they write, or *My selfish, self-centred behaviour embarrasses me now.*

Stop! I'm tempted to bring a foam baseball bat to class, so writers can get the violence of self-blame out of the way by bashing themselves over the head and then get back to showing us what happened. I do not want to read your recriminations, to go through your therapy. I want a reliable narrator not blinded by guilt or regret or rage to tell me a compelling tale.

Give an honest account and let the reader be the judge. Get out of the way of your own story.

Sometimes, though, if you simply cannot manage that—well, a little professional counselling by a skilled, compassionate, insightful professional might not hurt.

A relative of mine calls my work "dwelling." "Why do you keep dwelling in the past?" he says.

"Because that's my job," I reply. And I think but do not say, "You could use a bit of dwelling yourself, my friend."

What are your painful stories? Are you ready to set them free? Do you dare?

We are healed of a suffering only by expressing it to the full.

MARCEL PROUST

Childhood memories are sometimes covered and obscured beneath the things that come later, like childhood toys forgotten at the bottom of a crammed adult closet, but they are never lost for good.

NEIL GAIMAN

38

Determine what your story is really about

e♥

In Step 19, I wrote about Mary and the chocolate box that passed her by. When asked, "What is your story really about?" Mary replied, "My childhood during the war." But her story actually went far deeper to something more universal: the tale of an unloved child singled out by a parent for scorn and neglect. Deep inside, Mary knew that's what she was talking about; she just couldn't admit it. Once she recognized her real subject, she was able to refashion the story, which needed to start and end not with the war, but with her relationship with her difficult mother.

The most important question I ask in class is, "What is this story really about?" Often we can't see the answer ourselves. The story has one or more suitcases that need to be unpacked, revealing the key to the drama. That's why we write a loose, baggy first draft, pouring it all in—so we can get to the end and find out what's there and where we're really going. And that's why we usually need another eye: an editor, a class, a writing coach. Because sometimes we simply cannot see, from inside, which suitcase we are ignoring, what story we are actually trying to tell.

What's certain is that the important stories will eventually force themselves out, especially the ones we're doing our best to conceal.

When you've finished a draft, put your story away for a while. When you reread it, ask yourself, "What is this story really about? What is the journey? What is the moment of reflection or change?" A vital corollary to these questions is, "With this material, what is the most important story I can tell?"

Why stay on the surface? You want to write something that matters. Is your story really about the sweaty fun of playing softball as an adult, chuckling as you miss the ball? As you played, you remembered being a clumsy outsider as a kid, never chosen for the team, never good enough. Isn't that what your story is really about? Write the story that goes deep.

This does not mean all your stories have to be about trauma or unhappiness; not at all. E.B. White wrote about the most important and universal subjects: family, love, aging, nature, death. And yet his stories, written from the heart, are told with affection, wry humour, and joy.

Remember that, when you figure out what your story is really about, you want to give us a hint, even the barest clue, at the beginning. You want to make a promise the rest of your story is going to keep, so we'll come with you.

But just deciding to go deep is not enough. You have to know how to turn your most challenging experiences into readable prose, which is why it is important to ...

39

Write from scars,
not from wounds

❧

Some years ago, I participated in a month-long workshop for non-fiction writers at the Banff Centre for the Arts in Alberta, a glorious place and an invaluable resource for artists (suggestion—check it out at www.banffcentre. ca). In our group was a gifted young writer with a huge vocabulary and a unique style, but whose essay about her dysfunctional childhood was a hard-to-read cry of pain. She had opened doors; in fact, her doors were hanging off their hinges. We didn't know how to handle her agonized work. One colleague simply prepared a list of books for her about childhood abuse and therapy.

Our brilliant head editor explained that despite the writer's obvious talent, her pain had not healed enough for her to process the past and turn it into literature. She was writing not from scars, but from wounds.

When a student describes a powerful experience in an essay in class, we the listeners can sometimes fit ourselves right into the tale. We not only understand what the writer has been through, we feel we have, in our own, very different way, been through something like it as well. And other times, when a student presents such an experience, we shut down, because we can't tell what the story has to do with us.

The first writer has been able to stand far enough back to turn the experience into good writing. Raw emotion has healed enough to become a scar. The second writer is still coping with an open wound. We don't see or hear the pictures, the characters, or the story. We register only the intensity of the feelings.

A writer cannot create literature while dealing with strong emotions that have not been processed.

It's not just pain a writer needs to stand back from, but also love. If you rhapsodize with gooey ardour about your adorable children or your faultless parents, I'll close the book. I want a reliable narrator, not one swimming in out-of-control, over-the-top feelings, whether negative or positive. When emotion overwhelms a writer, he or she has proven to be an unreliable narrator. Readers are not sure they can trust such a narrator to lead them safely forward and tell them the truth.

Some do get away with writing from wounds. In *By Grand Central Station I Sat Down and Wept*, Elizabeth

Smart uses her fury and grief to create a masterpiece about the madness of obsessive love. Many readers admire the book; others, including me, do not. It's true a writer needs to mine that intense place of unprocessed emotion. But it's only later, when the rawness has healed enough for the emotion to be digested, that great writing for other eyes can emerge. In *The Year of Magical Thinking*, Joan Didion, writing just after the sudden death of her husband, evinces searing pain, but her expert clarity and skill as an essayist pull us into the cool clear heart of her loss.

When experience is new and burning, a journal is a most satisfactory friend. You are writing to understand, perhaps to heal, comfort, and validate yourself. But to write successfully for others to understand, you'll most likely have to wait until your wound becomes a scar. When will that happen? There's no way to know. Some wounds heal quickly; others take a very long time.

So how do writers move in close enough to their rich, emotional raw material to recreate it with genuine feeling and flow? And yet not move in so close that they are capsized by the original emotions all over again? How do they withdraw far enough to write about their most formidable experiences and yet still bring them vividly to life? Negotiating this precise distance is one of the memoirist's greatest challenges.

And what about other kinds of fiercely personal expression: ranting, musing, and confessing? How do we fit them into our work?

A rant, as CBC's Rick Mercer has shown us, is a relentless discourse, an objection to something or someone. It is often eloquent and entertaining, especially if we agree with it. But a rant on paper can produce the same reaction as writing from emotional wounds: All we can hear is fury, sarcasm, loathing.

Musing is an exploration of ideas, thoughts, dreams, fancies, memories—ideal for your journal and wonderful raw material for later work but often too unformed to be read by others. Essays and stories are crafted for readers; musing is not.

Again, beware abstract words: glory, loneliness, peace, heaven, heartache. They're powerful words, but I can't see them. A sudden kiss, a solitary walk in the woods, a break-up done by e-mail: These are concrete. They show where the abstract words of musing only tell. Pull me in with specifics and detail.

What's the difference between a memoir piece that tells the truth and a confession? Once more, it's the issue of wounds and scars, and also of craft. Many confessions are soul-wrenching truth-tellings, blurted outpourings that are undigested and unshaped. Good for diaries, good for spiritual counsellors, best friends, and shrinks, but not for readers. Not yet.

In your early drafts, pour out all the emotion you want and need. Later, pare back and prune. Remember that, when you are dealing with huge issues, the drama is there in the action on the page; you don't need to hit us with it. The more powerful the story, the greater the need to temper your tone. Keep your language spare and simple. Don't tell us what to feel. Make us see.

When you begin to write, ask yourself, "Do I feel in control of the material, or is the subject controlling me?" That might give you a hint about how far you have come and how far you have still to go.

There is something beautiful about all scars of whatever nature. A scar means the hurt is over, the wound is closed and healed, done with.

HARRY CREWS

If you have no wounds how can you know if you're alive? If you have no scar how do you know who you are?

EDWARD ALBEE

Ursula K. Le Guin, when dealing with painful subjects, makes a distinction between "wallowing," which she says she writes but does not share publicly, and "bearing witness," which she does.

JUDITH BARRINGTON

40

Be concerned about discretion

We live in an age in which people like to expose sensational truths, not just in print but also on television and all over the Internet. As you may have sensed by now, I believe in telling the truth. But I also believe in discretion, especially in any story that involves children or other vulnerable people. I cancelled my subscription to *Toronto Life* magazine when it published an article about the hideous divorce of what turned out to be the author's boyfriend and even included a colour picture of his children. I think the writer crossed the boundaries of taste and discretion. Many disagree. She won a National Magazine Award for the piece.

Once when a young woman read us a haunting, beautifully written essay about being sexually abused as a child by her grandfather, I asked if she would consider publishing it. "Only after my grandma dies," she said. "I don't care about him, but going public with this would kill her." I think that's the right answer. You should unpack the suitcases and tell the stories. But sometimes you don't need to put them out for public consumption right away, if ever.

There's a fine line between exposing a festering secret—unpacking—and making public a truth that may free the writer but harm innocent others. There's also the question of libel—of whether, in painting a negative portrait of someone recognizable, you open yourself to the risk of a lawsuit. If you think that may be a problem, change the names and disguise distinguishing characteristics (as I have of the students mentioned in this book); if you have any doubt, check with a lawyer.

You'll have to define your own boundaries, your standards of taste, risk-taking, and discretion, and there are instances where your lawyer may have ideas, too. For those who are comfortable giving out all kinds of personal details, the level of discomfort is very low. For others, who want to reveal little, extremely high.

Long after his death, I wrote an essay about my dad, which, after many tears, told some of the truth: Though a marvellous man, he was an angry, unskilled father who in my early years hurt me deeply. (This was before my trip to Siena.) When the essay was accepted by a respected literary magazine, as a courtesy before it appeared, I sent it to my mother. She was outraged at what it revealed and insisted it not be published. I pulled it.

I don't regret that decision now, not because I complied in keeping a family secret, but the reverse: I was not ready to tell the truth, the whole truth, and nothing but the truth.

My mother died not long ago, and now I feel released to tell the real family story of pain, redemption, and the blessings of maturity. I wrote as truthfully as I could while she was alive, but I didn't want anything to appear in print that would hurt her.

Was that cowardly? Yes and no. Kathryn Harrison went ahead and in *The Kiss* wrote an almost unbearably frank exposé of an incestuous affair she had as an adult with her previously estranged father. She later said that though she was glad to have written the book and told the truth, she was devastated by the violence of the critical reaction to her revelations. I admire her very brave work but doubt I could have gone that far myself.

A writer in England was condemned for publishing a tell-all memoir about her teenaged son's drug problem; the young man was devastated. I have never published anything about my children without their approval. Perhaps for the worse in my work, but not in my life.

Anne Lamott joked that she can think of no better reason to write than out of revenge. Is she right? I'm not sure; it depends. Others obviously agree, including David Sedaris, one of my favourite writers, whose unflinching eye for satirical veracity must alarm everyone who knows him.

What do you think? Do you have a story that would

hurt others if you published it? What will you do? There's an excellent book on this topic: *Family Trouble: Memoirists on the Hazards and Rewards of Revealing Family*, edited and with an introduction by Joy Castro. Find out how others have dealt with this issue.

Sometimes we need to tell the truth without worrying about protecting others. Sometimes we do not. It can be a difficult choice, but the choice is yours. You must decide the kind of writer you want to be.

The first quote below is from a courageous Nobel-prize winning writer, but in this instance, I do not entirely agree with her.

Write as though everyone you know is dead.

NADINE GORDIMER

My final recommendations are:

Befriend only people who are too poor to hire lawyers to sue you.

If you plan to write about friendship, make lots of friends, because you are bound to lose a few.

For the same reason, try to come from a large family.

PHILIP LOPATE

41

Take your time

A retired engineer in my class asked me to summarize my lectures so he could finish more quickly. He wanted lists of things to do, books to read, rules he could memorize so he could become a skilled and published writer immediately. Others, while not quite so impatient, have conveyed the same attitude: How quickly can I get through this to the finish line? Chop-chop. No time to waste.

Wayson tells a parable of an impatient young Hindu who goes to a famous guru with a request.

"Master, I want to become a great guru like you. If I study with you, how long will that take?"

"About ten years," replies the Master.

"Such a long time?" cries the young man. "What if I study with you during the day and read all the learned books through the night?"

"Well, then, I think it would take about twenty years," comes the reply.

The student doesn't understand.

"What if I read at night and study with you and also with another guru, so I get a double dose of non-stop teaching? How long then?"

"Then, my son," says the guru, "I think that would take about … thirty years."

Some things cannot be rushed, and enlightenment is one of them. Fundamental realizations and new skills take time, as well as hard work, study, focus, and practice. I tell my more driven students that creative achievement is different from anything else they've done. If a determined, disciplined person wants to learn how to play the tuba or climb Mount Everest, there are steps to take, and with application, determination, and sweat, success will almost inevitably follow.

The journey to good creative writing, however, is convoluted and fraught, and there is no guarantee of "success." Yes, we can practice and prepare: write a lot, read a lot, take classes, learn to edit and punctuate. But besides talent, there are other vital elements like courage and wisdom and the humility, self-knowledge, and self-confidence that illuminate a powerful narrative voice, which may come more slowly and cannot be forced. You may have Zen moments, instant flashes of enlightenment, but they will only come through hours of effort. It is a long, slow, sometimes tedious, and often painful journey.

To a sensible person, the question arises: Why bother? Well—because we're the kind of people who need to tell stories whether anyone is listening or not, and certainly whether anyone will pay to listen or not. That is the only reason, in the end, to proceed. Money is certainly no reason (see Step 47), and neither is fame. All we can do is learn to tell, as clearly and honestly as we can, the kinds of stories we ourselves like to hear. But getting to that kind of bravery, that openness, clarity, simplicity, and skill, can take a great deal of time.

Ironically, the writers with sensitivity and insight are often so self-deprecating and honest that they are easily silenced. I hope this does not include you. (If it does, please review Step 13.)

The whole problem with the world is that fools and fanatics are always so certain of themselves, and wiser people so full of doubts.

BERTRAND RUSSELL

Genius is eternal patience.

MICHELANGELO

You don't even have to know how or in what way, but if you are writing the clearest, truest words you can find and doing the best you can to understand and communicate, this will shine on paper like its own little lighthouse. Lighthouses don't go running all over an island looking for boats to save; they just stand there shining.

ANNE LAMOTT

42

Chart your course
from one to ten

❧

A friend of a friend called me recently.

"My son writes really good poetry, plays, and fantasy fiction," she said, "and he needs a publisher. How can he find one?"

Her son is nineteen. I've received this query a lot from students who want to be published. They look around at a world flooded with magazines, newspapers, books, and screenplays and wonder why their work shouldn't be part of that flood.

The answer? Because, almost always, they aren't ready yet. An acquaintance self-published a thousand copies of his novel, expecting it to find an audience—his wife and kids loved it—but it was so full of grammatical and structural mistakes, it was unreadable to a non-relative. He didn't understand that there are steps to go through, basic lessons that must be learned, before publishing.

Wayson has come up with a graphic way to explain the process of learning to write, charted as a journey from One to Ten. One is the start of the road, the desire to read, and Ten is the very end, being read after, even long after, your death. And Ten doesn't have to mean a famous dead writer like Tolstoy or Sylvia Plath. It could be a grandfather who wrote a beautiful diary like the one I read in Cape Breton, or a friend who sent you such a moving letter before she died that you reread it regularly. These writers are also at Ten.

One, the beginning, is loving to read. Nearly all writers start here. Two, the next step, is telling stories and weaving narratives. And Three is thinking, "I want to write. Maybe I should learn how." Everyone who comes to a writing class is at least at Three.

The problem is that Six, often, is where they want to be, instantly. Six is being published, "successfully" or not. John Grisham and Danielle Steel, with all their fame and wealth, are at Six, and so is the writer of a story in a community newspaper or a poet whose chapbook sells two hundred copies. Those who want to publish right away are anxious to jump from Three to Six.

But they've neglected to pass through Four, which is learning technique and craft, and Five, finding their true voice and developing their own style. It's necessary to attain these technical levels before considering publication, so you know exactly what you're doing on the page. Even at Three, getting started, you should know the fundamentals of grammar and punctuation. (As stated in Step 36, if this is your weak point, please don't let concern about bad grammar keep you from starting; however, you will have to address this issue eventually. There are books and courses to help you.)

At Four, you are learning narrative techniques, sentence structure and variety, and the kind of cutting and reworking that helps a writer be a good editor. At Five, you are probably reading constantly, absorbing the sentence rhythm, choice of vocabulary, and aesthetic effects of the masters while you work on and play with your own. As you move through these technical stages, you are figuring out your own narrative voice and how it works.

By Six, you've mastered a lot of the tools and tricks. Some writers, even as young as Anne Frank, will move quickly through those stages; they were well taught at school or their instincts are solid. Others will proceed much more slowly. There is no hurry; you cannot rush through Four, Five, and Six. It takes time to learn how you function creatively: your strengths and how to capitalize on them, your weaknesses and how to fix them. And exactly what a semicolon is and does (suggestion—find out).

At Six, your books may be found at airports or on newsstands or on websites or in obscure bookstores. You can stay right there, or you can continue on to Seven, Eight, and Nine. Literary writers work at these deeper levels, producing a profound, lasting product. Whereas Six writers are content to stay on the surface, literary writers move inward toward universal truths, mining their own depths, going further into human experience, into spiritual risk. Stephen King is a writer who usually works, with great skill and phenomenal success, at Six. But in *On Writing*, he speaks honestly, with gravitas and humour, about his life and work. In this book, he has moved to Seven or Eight. At Eight, Wayson says, you are working at such a meaningful, almost mystical level that you sometimes tremble as you write.

A writer working at Nine is as good as a living writer can be. One of the greatest of my Nine authors, the brilliant Canadian Alice Munro, winner of the Nobel Prize, produces stories of extraordinary precision, candour, and insight. (Suggestion—read her; then read her again.) Who are your Nine writers? And who are your Tens, the great writers who are no longer with us in body? Why these particular artists?

There is nothing inferior about working at Six; the writing is often solid and satisfying. And frankly, the higher you go, the less likely you are to make a good living, a few stars excepted; writers at Six have more popular appeal. But Seven, Eight, and Nine are where the greatest resonance and humanity are found. These books matter, and they will endure.

Be realistic about where you are now on your own journey. There's no stigma in being at Three or Four. You are learning and progressing with everything you write.

First, as with any art form, know thyself.

Where are you now, on a scale of one to ten?

1 ———————————————— 5 ———————————————— 10

Writers, more than other artists, seem to expect of themselves instant expertise. Perhaps this is because we all use words in everyday life, whereas we don't all use violins or oil paints. With other art forms, it is more obvious that there must be a long apprenticeship.

JUDITH BARRINGTON

43

Finish

There are many ways to sabotage yourself as a writer. Not beginning is one of the best. Petering out is another. Some writers work diligently until near the end of the process but simply cannot bring themselves to finish: to write an ending, edit, and then get the product out to the world or even to one reader. They want to write, and so they write. But if they never finish, they never have to deal with the next essential step, being read. They shut out the cruel possibility of a loved one's critique, a publisher's rejection, an editor's demands, a reviewer's snide comments, or even their own negative assessment.

Put the work away in a drawer almost but not quite finished, and you can live with the myth that it's brilliant but unpublished; that you are brilliant but unrecognized. That you're a good writer but just too damn busy to get the acclaim you deserve.

This kind of reasoning is common. Along with lack of confidence, stamina, and focus, perfectionism is another good way to block creative work: If I can't be the very best, it's not worth even trying. If I can't win the race, it's not worth running. Even if running itself, not the gold medal, is the joy.

But writing is not about racing to the finish line. It's about finishing the line on the page and writing the next one and the next, however long it takes, until the end. And then figuring out where the story should go.

One way to help yourself keep working is to set deadlines, even if they're arbitrary and artificial. Otherwise, who cares if you finish? Find a class. Besides providing structure and feedback, registering for a class means that if you don't do the work, you're throwing away your money. Find out about writing competitions from the Web or a local writers' organization, then send in your money and enter. Contest deadlines will force you to set a goal and stick to it.

Make a promise: By next Friday I will finish this story, I will mail in three pieces, I'll call the editor to find out what has happened to my proposal. Make this commitment publicly to your writing class or your writing partner. And do it.

Do not give up, please. So many become discouraged. No one ever said this kind of artistry would be easy. Facing rejection and criticism is as hard as writing; it's understandable to want to keep the work to yourself. But that's defeating the purpose. Surely you want to share what you've done, even with family and friends or with one special person. **Keep going until you write "The End." And then put it away and reread and revise and write it again. And then push it out.**

How do we know when a writing project is actually complete? Even after a piece of work has been published, writers want to go on fiddling. Editor Ellen Seligman once said, "A piece of writing is never finished. It is finished enough." For myself, I know a piece is done, for now, when it's clear that if I look at it once more, I'm going to throw up. Time to send the offspring out into the world.

The unread story is not a story. It's little black marks on wood pulp.

URSULA K. LE GUIN

One of the few things I know about writing is this: spend it all, play it, lose it, all, right away, every time ... Something more will arise for later, something better.

ANNIE DILLARD

QUESTIONS TO ASK

Things to think about as you begin, rework, and prepare to send out.

Getting ready:

Have I found a time, a place, and a routine for writing?

Have I assembled the tools that help me work?

Have I been able to make time for mulling? For reading like a writer?

Am I protecting my creative self by keeping the work to myself, at least at the beginning?

Am I beginning to figure out which are the vital stories I want to tell?

Starting to work:

Do I feel free to throw everything into the messy handbag of the first draft?

Do I start anywhere, knowing that I can always go back and change the beginning?

Have I broken the story into specific, detailed scenes?

Am I working toward a moment of clarity or change?

Am I as narrator often in the thick of the action, dramatizing, showing rather than telling the reader what my story entails?

Am I putting down my own truth my own way, as deeply and honestly as I can?

Am I brave enough to unpack my suitcases?

Have I done some research, if needed, to enrich the story with fact and detail?

Does my story paint pictures with vivid detail? With
dialogue?

Does my prose use simple rather than convoluted language?

Only the necessary adjectives and adverbs, similes and
metaphors?

Have I checked for clichés?

Have I checked for snags?

Have I checked for runways?

Have I checked for bows?

If I have a message, can I weave it into the showing of the
story rather than lecturing?

Am I avoiding conflict by being nice?

Are there suitcases to unpack?

Going deeper:

Have I had the courage to reveal my most important
stories? To risk?

Have I reread the draft and asked: What is this story really
about?

What is the most important story I can tell with this
material?

What is the journey?

What is the moment of change or reflection?

Am I in control of the material or is it controlling me?

Am I ranting, musing, confessing? If so, can I just share the
story instead?

Have I made a decision about how far I'll go in exposing
others in this tale?

Have I pushed through to some kind of ending?

Have I begun the lengthy, rewarding process of revision?

How much can I cut?

Is this piece of work ready to go out into the world in some
way? If so, where?

What should I write next?

And most importantly, what's for lunch?

THE WRITING
LIFE

44

Join a writers' group
or class

༄

Writing is a lonely business, particularly at the beginning, before you've had the encouragement and validation of publication. That's one good reason to find a good writing class—not just for the advice of the teacher but also for the companionship of the other students, fellow travellers on the journey to craft and truth. One of my goals as a writing teacher is to encourage students to bond into a group that will continue to meet for support and inspiration after the end of term.

Find at least one person who cares about you as a creative artist. It helps to know that someone else is aware of your struggles and your deadlines; that another trusted mind will listen to or read your work, as you will theirs.

You don't need a big group. Even one person will do, if it's the right person—someone who validates you and helps you stick with the work and grow.

And who knows what other benefits will arise? Five women from one of my classes went on meeting once a month for years, reading new work to one another. When Liz died suddenly at only fifty-eight, the others were shattered. While they mourned, they asked Liz's husband for permission to open her computer writing files. They chose two dozen of her stories, founded a publishing company, and edited, designed, and published a beautiful book of Liz's stories. How moved her family and friends were to have this memento of Liz's creativity. And at the time of this writing, the remaining four are meeting still.

Important note: I've heard of classes where students are diminished and criticized so harshly that they give up. If, in your class, you receive a critique of your work that's not constructive and that damages you, get out. Encouraging a competitive instead of a generous spirit in the classroom is, I think, the wrong way to teach creative writing.

However, at the same time, it's almost guaranteed you'll hear things you don't want to hear about how to improve your work. If you never receive a critical word, perhaps the teacher is not doing his job. And if you can't bear to hear his criticism, perhaps you're in the wrong field.

If you are stuck and don't have an encouraging class or group, there are other options: Go to the writing section of your local bookstore and pick through the slew of fantastic books about writing that provide cheerful backup and plenty of practical advice. (Some are listed at the back of this book.) And now there are many online writers' websites that list addresses of magazines, details of contests, advice, blogs, discussions … a world you can enter just sitting at your desk.

Cautionary note re "a world you can enter just sitting at your desk": The ease of e-mailing and Web surfing is a problem for many, if not most writers. It's tempting to think you're working—your fingers are moving over the keys, aren't they?—while in fact you're telling your fashionista friend about your new boots. Or you're busy reading about writing, which is not, repeat not, the same as actually writing.

When you're working, DISCONNECT. But spending time later with a creative friend or group, listening to new pieces, giving feedback, monitoring progress—that is a good use of your time.

Forget your generalized audience. In the first place, the nameless, faceless audience will scare you to death and in the second place, unlike the theater, it doesn't exist. In writing, your audience

is one single reader. I have found that sometimes it helps to pick out one person—a real person you know, or an imagined person and write to that one.

JOHN STEINBECK

45

Enter the marketplace

❧

Now you feel ready to take your work outside your writing space into the sharp air of the real reading world. In Canada, "Facts and Arguments," the daily personal essay in the *Globe and Mail* newspaper, is open to everyone. What a concept! The editors fill half a page for free, and ordinary writing citizens are published in a newspaper that lands on many thousands of doorsteps and on the Web, too. I started there decades ago with one piece and then many more, until I self-published a book of my *Globe* and CBC essays. Check the paper's website to find out the name of the current editor and the latest specifications and submit your best piece with a short note to the editor.

Go on. I dare you. What's the worst that can happen? That the piece won't run. Try again. The page has its ups and downs. You can be one of the ups.

"Lives Lived," the *Globe* obituary column, allows you to pay tribute to the recently departed while trying to compress an entire life into five hundred words. (More detailed info may be found at the back of this book.)

CBC Radio has fewer spots for personal essays than it used to, but there are still a few, like *The Sunday Edition*. Other radio stations have open spots; listen for them.

Competitions give you a deadline, force you to finish and mail something, and who knows? Maybe you'll be the chosen one. At least you'll have finished a piece you can send elsewhere. Look online for websites that list competitions.

One student, a brain surgeon, was an aggressive marketer of his writing. He published essays regularly about his medical work and also found a dog magazine interested in articles about his beloved beagles. It's practically guaranteed that there's a magazine devoted to your area of expertise or hobby or obsession and in need of material; look at their specifications online.

Go to a good, preferably independent, bookstore—please support those rare birds that remain—and check out literary magazines, where many novice writers start. Some of the best in Canada are *The Walrus*, *Geist*, *Brick*, *Event*, *Exile*, and *Maisonneuve*, but there are many more.

Don't forget free neighbourhood newspapers, which are always hungry for content. They may be humble and pay little or nothing, but your neighbours will read your work and see you're a published writer. Don't be a snob about the placement of your first efforts.

Please do not be put off by rejection. (I know, I know: easy to say.) Constant rejection is the experience of all artists. One example: At the beginning of my career, I sent a long profile of a brilliant teacher to a parenting magazine. Now I know that, before doing that kind of exhaustive work, I should have submitted a proposal and signed a contract, but I was new and eager to be heard.

A writer friend happened to interview the editor at the time and mentioned my name.

"Oh yes—her piece was on my desk," said the editor, "and I threw it out."

She threw it out because she didn't know me, and who knows, maybe she had a headache that day. It happens. She fished it from her garbage pail, liked it a lot, and ran it.

If a piece comes back once or twice, send it somewhere else. If it comes back three times, take a good hard look and revise it thoroughly. Then send it out again. There is no place for sensitive feelings on the business end of the creative writing trade. Get over them and move on.

If you want to publish a book of essays or a memoir, one of critical first steps is to craft the right letter to an agent or publishing house. The query letter is intended to push open the door and show you're a serious writer worth an investment of time and money. Getting the query letter right is so important, there are books about how to do just that. I recommend reading one or consulting an expert before you move ahead.

I realize I haven't spoken much about webzines or other online sites for writers. That's because, as someone born in the middle of the last century (1950—prehistory!), it's still more natural for me to deal with paper than with the electronic ozone on the other side of the screen. Please rectify this deficit for yourself. There not only are countless sites with great reading and information, but there also are many to which you can submit your work.

I don't teach writing. I teach patience. Toughness. Stubbornness. The willingness to fail. I teach the life.

RICHARD BAUSCH

46

Consider self-publication

Oh the shame! A real publisher doesn't want your work, so you have to publish it yourself. How humiliating.

Try telling that to the thousands who now self-publish to great effect and even great profit. These days it's more difficult than ever to get through to the big publishing houses or even the small ones, especially with hard-to-market products like a book of essays or a memoir by someone without a platform. A platform, as one publisher told me, means "you're already famous or connected—Britney Spears's mother did not have trouble getting a memoir published—or you've endured some hideous disaster." Despite the success of bestsellers like Cheryl Strayed's *Wild*, a formidable book about a feat of extreme endurance by a previously unknown writer, it's almost impossible to find a publisher for what's called a "nobody memoir."

Many nobodies, including your humble correspondent, have simply decided to pay to get their work edited, designed, typeset, printed, bound, and distributed, hoping to sell enough at least to break even. I did this with my previous book, a memoir, as well as with this one. The process is remarkably fast and easy, it's relatively inexpensive, and there's no stigma any more. Self-publishing has to do, not with lack of talent or commercial potential, but with impatience to see the work in completed form and desire to control both production and profits.

Google "self-publishing" to find sites in your area or even on the other side of the world. You'll need to make sure the work is properly edited and formatted first, but that should be done anyway. And then, unless you're convinced of the literary value of your opus and sure a publisher will be interested, make yourself a book. It won't preclude sending the work to a publisher, too.

Books, including self-published ones, last forever.

Early in the creative process, an easy way to turn your scattered pile of printed pages into the semblance of a published book is to punch holes in them and store them in a binder. This will instantly turn an early draft into a book. You can read your stories through, rearrange your chapters, see what fits and what doesn't, and all with a simple three-dollar, three-ring binder. The manuscript pages of this book were in one for years.

The rub for writers these days, whether self-published or with a publishing house, is the need to be instrumental in the marketing of our books. It's not enough that we wrote the @!$# thing, we have to help sell it, too. This is especially true when self-publishing. A command of social media is invaluable.

However, the process is arduous and the outcome always uncertain. I showed the manuscript of my memoir *All My Loving,* the story of my imaginary love affair as a young teen with Beatle Paul McCartney, to a book publicist. She told me that because I'm not famous and the book is a mere saga about life in the Sixties and the importance of the Beatles, she could not help me with publicity.

"Now, if you'd actually slept with Paul McCartney," she said, "it would be different."

Indeed, I thought. It certainly would.

Like any art, memory and memoir are meant to go public, no matter how personal, no matter how small.

RIGOBERTO GONZALES

47

Forget about money, fame, and bestsellers

e⌒

If you're a new writer, you need to keep one symbol firmly in mind. It resembles a "do not enter" sign, but it's a big black dollar sign with an even bigger red line running right through it.

People from the real world of nine to five have a hard time comprehending just how little money there is in most creative writing. You point to Harry Potter's J.K. Rowling, the richest writer in the world. And I point to thousands of writers, just as skilled, hard-working, and talented, who did not achieve great popularity and go on to break worldwide records or even get published at all.

Rowling took a huge and courageous risk. A single mother on government support, she used part of her welfare money for babysitting so she could sit in a café inventing a world of wizards, wands, and flying broomsticks—how's that for crazy? Any sane person would have gone out to get a job. But she was determined, and she was lucky; though her manuscript was rejected many times, eventually she hit it very, very big. Most of us won't even come close.

How much money do I make each year from writing? Of course it ebbs and flows a great deal depending on what phase of the process I'm in, but recently, about $600 a year. Yes, hard as it is to believe, I call myself a writer and some years that's all I've earned from my profession. My first book, which, as mentioned in the Introduction, is a biography of my great-grandfather the "Jewish Shakespeare," took me more than twenty years, on and off, to research and to write; it was published by an American university press. I calculate that the book cost me over $200,000 in lost income and actual expenses over two decades. Recently, the publisher sent me last year's royalty cheque—for $88. At least it was $88 U.S. I was happy to get it. Once they sent an accounting form that said the year's sales had brought in minus $17. I laughed until I cried.

For years, I got by on child support because my ex-husband was paying the mortgage.

The money I live on now comes not from writing, obviously, but from teaching writing at two universities, editing and coaching writers privately, and renting out rooms in my house. (Though soon, undoubtedly, I'll earn a vast fortune from the proceeds of this book and have to rewrite this page! A new step will be needed: Step 51—Learn to Cope with Wealth and Fame. Hope, goes the cliché, springs eternal.)

Some writers spend a lot of time writing grant proposals, or they drive cabs or do PR or advertising or speech writing or ghost writing or other kinds of writing for hire. Professionals divide work into the scribbling that pays the bills and the scribbling they do for the soul, which may never bring in a single penny. That's the risk they have to take—if they can afford to.

An article about earnings in the arts pointed out that a surprising number of writers, despite exceptionally low incomes, own their own homes. What this really means, the article concluded, is that their partners or parents or patrons have helped house them. Artists have always needed patrons; think of the Medicis, or of the faithful Theo van Gogh, who constantly sent money to keep his brother Vincent alive. It is possible to make a living as a freelance non-fiction writer, no question, if you hustle and schmooze and are as good or better at business and billing as you are at writing.

But if you're not, if you have a romantic notion of writing a great book no matter what the practical realities of the market, then make sure you're connected to someone employed or wealthy who loves you a lot and supports your dream, or else that you have a paying job or grant that will cover your living expenses. Remember Trollope: You can work full-time at the post office and write lots of books.

When doubt strikes, think of Vincent van Gogh. He didn't become an artist till he was in his mid-twenties and then taught himself with ferocious dedication to draw and paint. He was both a genius and a hard worker, and he was singularly unsuccessful commercially. If we judge him by the money he made, he's nothing. But his work has immeasurably enriched our planet—thanks to brother Theo.

All a writer really needs, says Orhan Pamuk, the Turkish Nobel Prize winner, is "paper, a pen, and the optimism of a child looking at the world for the first time."

Like Vincent.

When a writer wonders, "Will it sell?" he is lost, not because he is looking to make an extra buck or two, but rather because, by dint of asking the question in the first place, he has oriented himself toward the expectations of others. The world is not a focus group. The world is an appetite waiting to be defined.

ROGER ROSENBLATT

48

Relish your age

C rafting literature with skill and honesty is bloody hard work. "Writing is easy," a famous writer once said. "You just sit in front of a blank page and open a vein." Ha.

The good thing, however, is that you can open a vein at any age. You can spend your entire life doing something else and turn to creative work in the winter of your years. Or you can be young and have done little else so far. There's no age limit for the suffering, frustration, and slog of writing. Hooray!

Some writers, such as the astonishing Penelope Fitzgerald and Diana Athill (suggestion—read them), achieve bestseller status for the first time in late middle or even old age. My student Margaret Norquay published her moving first book, a memoir, when she was eighty-six. There are bloggers out there in their nineties and even their hundreds. Writing is not ballet or hockey. How lucky we scribblers are that our job does not require firm young biceps. Just a heart and a brain and a need to tell the tales of an eventful lifetime.

A writer—and, I believe, generally all persons— must think that whatever happens to him or her is a resource. All things have been given to us for a purpose, and an artist must feel this more intensely. All that happens to us, including our humiliations, our misfortunes, our embarrassments, all is given to us as raw material, as clay, so that we may shape our art.

JORGE LUIS BORGES

49

Cherish your body

ℰ

What is this chapter doing here? Who am I to tell you how to care for the physical plant that envelops your brain? I'll tell you who—once a cerebral, bookish kid whose only sport was ping-pong, then an adult who has never downhill skied. And yet not long ago I won the Senior Women's division of my neighbourhood's fund-raising Mini-Marathon. Okay, the key word is "mini"—one mile—and my category was so slow that I stopped to tie my shoelace and still won. But the point is that a buzzing mind on feeble legs claimed a brief moment of victory.

Writers are by definition not only solitary but immobile. Unless you are one of those rare writers—Dickens was one—who write standing up and pacing, your job is to sit, sometimes for hours a day. Your fingers are moving and your brain is overheated, but you are planted on a chair. One of the first rules of writing is BOC: bum on chair. That's how the work gets done. But what happens to the bum?

And when the writer does take a break and rise, it is natural to eat, and, yes, to drink and smoke. We ink-stained wretches tend to lack restraint when it comes to addictive mind-altering substances. Why is that? Perhaps the solitary, sedentary, and emotionally demanding nature of the profession, not to mention the financial vulnerability just discussed. And the fact that most of us begin to write because we are inordinately sensitive and sometimes even deranged to start with. We all know about great talents like Dylan Thomas, Dorothy Parker, and F. Scott Fitzgerald— brilliant creatures of excess who died far too young.

I have nothing to say about your alcohol or drug consumption (she said, downing her ubiquitous—a great five-dollar word—glass of red wine). But here is a piece of advice about your lifestyle: Move. Move your body. Exercise is good not only for your heart, lungs, and blood, your muscles and your mood, but also for your brain. It keeps your mind fresh. It keeps your body alive, rather than just a husk under the head that the hands grow from.

For many years I have attended the same fitness class at the YMCA, where someone tells me what to do so I can waddle behind like a duckling. Sometimes I chat with the others, enjoying a moment of contact in a solitary day. But other times, as I jog around in silence, I'm hit by some of my most interesting ideas. Things fall into place; new takes on the work fly down from the Y's brightly lit ceiling. I don't even notice that I'm sweating and my hamstrings hurt. I am thinking, yes, but on the move.

Keeping fit also means that when the time comes to do a reading or embark on a speaking tour or, God forbid, appear on television, all of which successful writers have to do, you will look perky and not wheeze.

Exercise is my medicine.

DAVID SUZUKI

50

Keep going

Please, don't be bound or hemmed in by the pointers in this book. One student, who had a very painful story to tell, was so worried she was writing from wounds rather than scars that she tried to create a scarring test to make sure she'd healed enough to tell her tale. Perhaps she's one of the people who will write magnificently from wounds. Who knows? I've given you guidelines, indicators, ideas, suggestions. None of these applies to Alice Munro. She finds her own way to and through a story, and so will you.

Every writer is different. We all know that, but it bears repeating. There is no right or wrong way to become a good writer, except not to start writing at all, not to persevere. To be silenced. That is the wrong way. The right way is, first, to make the effort to discover your own creative process, which almost certainly will be unlike any other writer's.

A great deal is packed into this dense little book, but a great deal more is missing. There's far more to learn about issues like voice, grammar, and structure, which other books handle well. (Suggestion: Go deeper. Find some of the books listed at the back at your local independent bookstore or library and absorb them.)

If this isn't enough help for you on your own, perhaps you need more detailed and directed guidance. There are skilled editors for hire out there; contact a local editing union or organization, such as the Editors' Association of Canada.

Find a way to get feedback and support for your efforts. Again, check out creative writing courses at schools, colleges, and universities, many of which offer degree or certificate programs or Continuing Education classes. If it's impossible for you to attend in person, look for courses offered online or by mail.

Please remember that the world is hungry for stories; the need for narrative may even be hardwired into our brains. Not long ago, people sat regularly around the dinner table talking about their days. Many went each week to a place of worship and chatted with each other and heard sermons that explored right and wrong. Now most of us, especially the young, spend our lives sitting alone, bombarded by pictures on screens and communicating through small, shiny magic devices. People want and need the honest personal voices missing in daily life. We turn to self-help books, television talk shows, and Internet sites to learn how to live, how to survive, how to prevail.

By making the effort to tell our own deepest truths, we are not writing just for ourselves. We are writing for others whom we want to reach. And for the world.

Write your pieces as you would write your lives— with restraint, precision, generosity toward every point of view including the wicked ones, and in the service of significant subject matter.

ROGER ROSENBLATT

What kind of attitude engenders lasting non-fiction? Terry Tempest Williams gives the best answer I've ever heard: "Deep commitment, deep patience, and deep passion."

PHILIP GERARD

Conclusion

This is where I leave you.

Now you have, I hope, some concept of the technical requirements of this job. You know something about the impediments, the Mr. Plouxes of negativity who will try to silence you, the difficulty and pleasure of staying on track, finishing, editing, sending out.

Perhaps I have not talked enough about the satisfaction of this work. With two jobs I love, I'm one of the luckiest people on earth. Teaching writing gives me an external challenge, a regular paycheque, and company. My own writing takes me inside to where my suitcases are still waiting to be unpacked, where my most meaningful thoughts reside. Those rare moments when words are flowing onto the page—bliss. At times like that, it's easy to forget the frustratingly slow birth of other work.

And then there's feedback. When an essay of mine about divorce ran in a newspaper one morning, I was up early reading my lovely words, gazing fondly at my lovely byline on the page as I always do and as I hope you will, too. The phone rang at seven o'clock that morning. It was a stranger calling from another city. "I hope you don't mind me tracking you down," he said, his voice breaking. "I just had to tell you that your piece this morning—that's me. That's my story."

But it wasn't. It was my story, which I'd tried to tell as clearly and honestly as I could, with whatever craft I could muster. I told one specific story about my own divorce, and someone had to call me because it was his story, too. That's what, at its best, makes the struggle worthwhile: We are trying to reach through the silence, to be heard, to make a difference. The joys of accomplishment and connection are huge.

Make a promise to your creative self and write it down. Keep it simple enough that you can actually achieve it: I will write every other day for a month. I will register for a class, read that book on grammar, contact that fellow writer and meet for coffee, mutual support, on-the-spot writing.

Make a promise you can keep, keep it, and then make another one.

Take what you've learned here and what you already

know about the world and about yourself. Find a time, a place, an instrument of notation, and a routine. Begin somewhere, without judgement, to tell a story that matters to you. Keep going, without judgement, taking all the time necessary. End somewhere.

Put it away for a while. Reread and see what hits you. Ask some questions: What is this really about? What is the journey? What is the moment of change? What is the most important story I can tell with this material?

Why am I telling this story? Can I summarize it in one line?

Do some reworking. Cut. Reread. Mull. Do some research. Go deeper. Dare to risk exploring the truth, being aware of the issue of wounds and scars. Keep your heart open open open. Read it aloud. Cut some more. Add a crucial new bit of context. Put it away again.

When you're not writing, pay attention to the life around you and to the life inside you and to the child you once were. Read a lot. Go for long walks in green leafy places and concrete ones, too. Look at paintings. Listen to music. Listen to your heart and mind.

When you've ripped apart and resewn your piece enough, find a reader you respect to have a look. Listen carefully for what's useful and what's not. Rewrite.

Is it ready to go out into the world? Where should it go? What a terrifying, exhilarating thought.

Congratulations. You're a writer.

For all its frailty and bitterness, the human heart is worthy of your love. Love it. Have faith in it. Both you and the human heart are full of sorrow. But only one of you can speak for that sorrow and ease its burdens and make it sing—word after word after word.

ROGER ROSENBLATT

P.S. More Wayson words

~ℰ∽

S ome years ago, I e-mailed Wayson that the chapters of my memoir were becoming episodic: "Then this happened, and then this and this."

This was his e-mail back:

> YES, you can do the best writing of your inner creative life!
>
> FOCUS, dear Beth—write about one of the most vulnerable and meaningful episodes that you can recall with enough clarity or emotion to RECREATE it into a work of creative non-fiction. You're an artist, not a recorder. WRITE THE DAMN THING AS IF YOUR LIFE DEPENDS UPON IT. Be messy, chaotic, but

never let go the truth of what you are feeling as you write. Do not think, think, THINK! Write relentlessly! Pour it all out. That's what I do.

Do ONLY the hot bits that burn your heart to this day—and as you use every bit of your craft to recreate the emotional realities of that experience, a flood of the most essential details will come to you (note: DETAILS, not "facts"). Free your deepest memory to express itself without any concern for facts.

It is emotional truth we are seeking, not a diary entry, an anecdote, or a journal of events. Surrender to the shaking self and write your heart out. Never mind any sequential or chronological details, correct names or even age! Hauntings are their own reality—and much more dramatic and inspiring. Fine-tune later. Get the MOST IMPORTANT, FRIGHTENING, JOYFUL, ECSTATIC, ENLIGHTENING, CHAOTIC, RAW moments out on paper. To quote a colleague of mine, "Memory, after all, is just another form of fiction."

FREE YOURSELF TO EXPRESS YOURSELF! Yes, a thousand times YES, you can write at that white-heat, enchanted, inspired depth. There, the best and rawest material is waiting for you.

xox Wayson

YES is a very good word. I needed to hear Wayson say it.

I hope you've heard it, too.

Here it is again, for you. Take it in and start.

YES.

And remember ... write about dogs.

Information on submitting essays and articles

Newspapers: *The Globe and Mail*—The editors change regularly. Check all details online.

- "Facts and Arguments"—An essay about a personal topic, about 900 words. Check for details at http://www.theglobeandmail.com/life/facts-and-arguments/submit-a-facts-and-argumentsessay/article597357. Send queries and essays to facts@globeandmail.com.
- "Lives Lived"—An obituary of about 500 words about someone who has died within the last six months. Again, check details online. Submit to lives@globeandmail.com.

Almost all newspapers run opinion pieces and even personal essays on their op-ed page or in longer weekend editions. Check for specifications. Local community newspapers and tabloids are always looking for material.

Radio: CBC Radio used to have lots of time for listener essays, much less now. Individual programs sometimes have calls for submissions, especially *The Sunday Edition* and *The Vinyl Cafe with Stuart McLean.*

Canadian general interest magazines—*Maclean's, Canadian Living, Canadian Geographic, Reader's Digest, Chatelaine, Today's Parent,* and many more. Check websites for contributor guidelines and send queries rather than whole pieces.

Canadian literary magazines—*Geist, Prism, Brick, The Fiddlehead, The Antigonish Review, Room Magazine, The Walrus, Prairie Fire, Event, Exile,* etc.

American literary magazines—*Tin House, The Sun, Topic, Creative Non-Fiction, Brevity,* many more.

Specialty magazines—Whatever you're an expert in or on, there's a magazine about it.

Websites—A huge ever-growing resource. Again, constantly changing, so use your Google fingers.

Look for lists of writing contests, such as the Event, the Edna Staebler, and the CBC creative non-fiction competitions. Enter! Visit writers' websites and blogs for encouragement, ideas, and gossip.

Selected books on writing

Books About Writing and Creativity

The Art of Time in Memoir: Then, Again, Sven Birkerts.

The Artist's Way: A Spiritual Path to Higher Creativity,
Julia Cameron.
A therapeutic workbook, not to everyone's taste, but
even if you find the "healing" aspects a bit laboured, the
practical suggestions and quotes are worth reading.

Becoming a Writer, Dorothea Brande.

*If You Want to Write: A Book About Art, Independence
and Spirit*, Brenda Ueland.
Two classic books from the Thirties that are sensible,
insightful, not dated despite their age.

Bird by Bird: Some Instructions on Writing and Life,
  Anne Lamott.
  Funny, chatty, full of heart and passion.

The Creative Habit: Learn It and Use It for Life, Twyla
  Tharp and Mark Reiter.
  A practical guide, with exercises, from a great
  choreographer.

*Creative Nonfiction: Researching and Crafting Stories of
  Real Life,* Philip Gerard.

*How to Become a Famous Writer Before You're Dead:
  Your Words in Print and Your Name in Lights,* Ariel
  Gore.

Into the Woods: How Stories Work and Why We Tell Them,
  John Yorke.

Inventing the Truth: The Art and Craft of Memoir,
  William Zinsser.
On Writing Well: The Classic Guide to Writing Nonfiction,
  William Zinsser.
Writing About Your Life: A Journey into the Past, William
  Zinsser.
  Three superb must-read books.

*The Joy of Writing: A Guide for Writers, Disguised as a
  Literary Memoir ...,* Pierre Berton.

*Keep It Real: Everything You Need to Know About
  Researching and Writing Creative Non-fiction,* Lee
  Gutkind, editor.

Long Quiet Highway: A Memoir on Zen in America and the Writing Life, Natalie Goldberg.

Wild Mind: Living the Writer's Life, Natalie Goldberg.

Writing Down the Bones: Freeing the Writer Within, Natalie Goldberg.
Some love her, some find her too "new agey," but she does challenge and stimulate. I think the first and third are the strongest.

The Making of a Story: A Norton Guide to Creative Writing, Alice LaPlante.
A classic.

Memoir: A History, Ben Yagoda.

One Writer's Beginnings, Eudora Welty.

Reading Like a Writer: A Guide for People Who Love Books and for Those Who Want to Write Them, Francine Prose.

Reality Hunger: A Manifesto, David Shields.

The Situation and the Story: The Art of Personal Narrative, Vivian Gornick.
Excellent.

So You Want to Write: How to Master the Craft of Writing Fiction and Memoir, Marge Piercy and Ira Wood.

The Sound on the Page: Great Writers Talk About Style and Voice in Writing, Ben Yagoda.

The Storytelling Animal: How Stories Make Us Human, Jonathan Gottschall.

Tell It Slant: Writing and Shaping Creative Nonfiction,
Brenda Miller and Suzanne Paolo.

*Telling True Stories: A Nonfiction Writers' Guide from
the Nieman Foundation at Harvard University*, Mark
Kramer and Wendy Call, editors.
More about journalism than creative non-fiction, but
interesting nonetheless.

*Unless It Moves the Human Heart: The Craft and Art of
Writing*, Roger Rosenblatt.
Beautiful.

*Why We Write: 20 Acclaimed Authors on How and
Why They Do What They Do*, Meredith Maran,
editor.

*The Writer as an Artist: A New Approach to Writing
Alone and with Others*, Pat Schneider.

*The Writer on Her Work: Seventeen Essays by Twentieth-
Century American Writers*, Janet Sternburg, editor.

A Writer's Life: The Margaret Laurence Lectures, Writers'
Trust of Canada.
Twenty-five well-known Canadian writers talk about
writing and life.

*Writing Creative Nonfiction: Instruction and Insights
from the Teachers of the Associated Writing
Programs*, Carolyn Forché and Philip Gerard, editors.
Essays on "the art, the craft, the business" and even
the reader.

Writing from Life: A Guide for Writing True Stories,
Heather Robertson.
An experienced Canadian journalist shares her
insights into the craft of non-fiction writing. Very
useful.

*Writing in a New Convertible with the Top Down:
A Unique Guide for Writers*, Sheila Bender and
Christi Killien.

Writing in General and the Short Story in Particular,
Rust Hills.

The Writing Life, Annie Dillard.
An opinionated, fierce, and talented writer talks about
her craft.

*Writing Life Stories: How to Make Memories into
Memoirs, Ideas into Essays and Life into Literature*,
Bill Roorbach with Kristen Keckler, PhD.
A superb book, warm, clear, down-to-earth.

Writing the Memoir: From Truth to Art, Judith Barrington.
Eight writers talk about delving into memoir.

*Writing on Both Sides of the Brain: Breakthrough
Techniques for People Who Write*, Henriette Anne
Klauser.
Another therapeutic workbook.

*Writing Past Dark: Envy, Fear, Distraction and Other
Dilemmas in the Writer's Life*, Bonnie Friedman.

Writing to Change the World, Mary Pipher.

Writing Tools: 50 Essential Strategies for Every Writer,
Roy Peter Clark.

*You Can't Make This Stuff Up: The Complete Guide
to Writing Creative Nonfiction—from Memoir to
Literary Journalism and Everything in Between,* Lee
Gutkind.
Practical, down to earth, invaluable.

You Should Really *Write a Book: How to Write, Sell and
Market Your Memoir,* Regina Brooks and Brenda Lane
Richardson.

Books of Essays and Interviews

*The Art of the Personal Essay: An Anthology from the
Classical Era to the Present,* selected by Phillip
Lopate.
A comprehensive, international compendium of
personal writing, from Seneca to the present.

The Best American Essays of the Century, Joyce Carol
Oates, editor.

The Best of Modern Humor, Mordecai Richler, editor.

*The Heart Does Break: Canadian Writers on Grief and
Mourning,* George Bowering and Jean Baird, editors.

Journeys: An Anthology, Robyn Davidson, editor.

*Just Enough Liebling: Classic Work by the Legendary
New Yorker Writer,* A.J. Liebling.

Modern American Memoirs, Annie Dillard and Cort
   Conley, editors.

The Moth: 50 True Stories, Catherine Burns, editor.

Original Minds, Eleanor Wachtel.
*Writers and Company: Conversations with CBC Radio's
   Eleanor Wachtel*, Eleanor Wachtel.
*More Writers and Company: New Conversations with
   CBC Radio's Eleanor Wachtel*, Eleanor Wachtel.
   Lucid, fascinating interviews with writers from her
   invaluable radio program, on CBC Radio One at 3 p.m.
   on Sunday.

Pulphead: Essays, John Jeremiah Sullivan.

This Is the Story of a Happy Marriage, Ann Patchett.
   Essays about writing and life.

Writers at Work: The Paris Review Interviews, George
   Plimpton, editor.

*Writing Life: Celebrated Canadian and International
   Authors on Writing and Life*, Constance Rooke, editor.

Books on Journal Writing
A Book of One's Own: People and Their Diaries, Thomas
   Mallon.
   An exhaustive study of diaries through the years,
   divided into categories such as "Travellers,"
   "Confessors," "Prisoners."

*The Assassin's Quote: An Anthology of the World's
Greatest Diarists*, Irene and Alan Taylor, editors.

The Hidden Writer: Diaries and the Creative Life,
Alexandra Johnson.
The "hidden writing" of creative women.

Our Private Lives: Journals, Notebooks, and Diaries,
Daniel Halpern, editor.
Excerpts from writers' diaries.

Books on Writing Technique and Getting Published
The Artful Edit: On the Practice of Editing Yourself,
Susan Bell.

The Elements of Style, William Strunk, Jr., E.B. White, and
Roger Angell.
The classic little volume about the rules of style.

*Grammatically Correct: The Essential Guide to Spelling,
Style, Usage, Grammar, and Punctuation*, Anne
Stilman.

*How to Get Happily Published: A Complete and Candid
Guide*, Judith Appelbaum.
Advice about the real world of publishing.

How to Write a Sentence: And How to Read One, Stanley
Fish.

*Thinking Like Your Editor: How to Write Great Serious
Nonfiction—and Get It Published*, Susan Rabiner and
Alfred Fortunato.

And

yes

True to Life: Fifty Steps to Help You Tell Your Story, Beth
Kaplan.
Brilliantly succinct. A must-read. Buy two.

Some recommended memoirs

(As soon as this list goes to the publisher, I know I'll remember forty wonderful books I've forgotten to include. My apologies to those writers. To you my readers: There are superb new works of creative non-fiction appearing every day. Check your newspaper or online for news and reviews, go to your local independent bookstore or library or one of the Internet sellers for copies, and READ THEM.)

Canadian
1982, Jian Ghomeshi.

Belonging: Home Away from Home, Isabel Huggan.
   Aching and warm.

Broad Is the Way: Stories from Mayerthorpe, Margaret
  Norquay.

The Concubine's Children, Denise Chong.

*The Danger Tree: Memory, War, and the Search for a
  Family's Past*, David Macfarlane.
  Beautiful prose.

Memoirs of Montparnasse, John Glassco.

The Mother Zone, Marni Jackson.
  Wryly funny.

My Turquoise Years: A Memoir, M.A.C. Farrant.

Not Yet: A Memoir of Living and Almost Dying, Wayson
  Choy.

Paper Shadows: A Chinatown Childhood, Wayson Choy.
  Haunting.

*Perfection of the Morning: A Woman's Awakening in
  Nature*, Sharon Butala.

*Raisins and Almonds: The Rich Memoir of a Childhood
  on the Canadian Prairies*, Fredelle Bruser Maynard.

Roughing It in the Bush, Susanna Moodie.

Running in the Family, Michael Ondaatje.
  A feast of prose.

Shadow Child: An Apprenticeship in Love and Loss, Beth
  Powning.

Something Fierce: Memoirs of a Revolutionary Daughter, Carmen Aguirre.

Thin Ice: Coming of Age in Canada, Bruce McCall.

Too Close to the Falls: A Memoir, Catherine Gildiner Quirky.

The Way of a Boy: A Memoir of Java, Ernest Hillen.

And

yes

All My Loving: Coming of Age with Paul McCartney in Paris, Beth Kaplan.
Brilliant, hilarious, compelling in every way. A must read. Buy three.

Other

Any non-fiction (almost) by E.B. White, M.F.K. Fisher, George Orwell, James Baldwin, Truman Capote, David Sedaris, Roger Rosenblatt. Anything at all by Chekhov, Mary Oliver, and Grace Paley—not strictly non-fiction writers, but the best.

Act One: An Autobiography, Moss Hart.

An American Childhood, Annie Dillard.

And When Did You Last See Your Father? A Son's Memoir of Love and Loss, Blake Morrison.
A short memoir turned into a film with Colin Firth.

Angela's Ashes: A Memoir, Frank McCourt.
Seminal Irish memoir of dysfunction.

Are You Somebody? The Accidental Memoir of a Dublin Woman, Nuala O'Faolain.
Almost There, Nuala O'Faolain.
Wonderfully rich, funny, and frank.

Autobiography of a Face, Lucy Grealy.

Bad Blood: A Memoir, Lorna Sage.

Blackbird: A Childhood Lost and Found, Jennifer Lauck.
The ultimate dysfunctional family.

Born Round: A Story of Family, Food and a Ferocious Appetite, Frank Bruni.

Borrowed Finery: A Memoir, Paula Fox.

The Boys of My Youth, Jo Ann Beard.
A classic, especially the essay "The Fourth State of Matter."

Cider with Rosie, Laurie Lee.

The Dharma Bums, Jack Kerouac.

Don't Get Too Comfortable: The Indignities of Coach Class, the Torments of Low Thread Count, the Never-Ending Quest for Artisanal Olive Oil, and Other First World Problems, David Rakoff.

Dreams from My Father: A Story of Race and Inheritance, Barack Obama.

The Duke of Deception: Memories of My Father, Geoffrey Wolff.

Eat, Pray, Love: One Woman's Search for Everything Across Italy, India, and Indonesia, Elizabeth Gilbert. A bestseller, and of course a film with Julia Roberts and the luscious Javier Bardem, be still my beating heart.

An Education, Lynn Barber. A short memoir turned into a film with Carey Mulligan.

Family Sayings, Natalia Ginzburg.

Fierce Attachments: A Memoir, Vivian Gornick.

The Flame Trees of Thika: Memories of an African Childhood, Elspeth Huxley.

The Flâneur: A Stroll Through the Paradoxes of Paris, Edmund White.

The Florist's Daughter: A Memoir, Patricia Hampl.

French Lessons: A Memoir, Alice Kaplan.

Fun Home: A Family Tragicomic, Alison Bechdel. A graphic memoir that has been turned into a musical.

Girl, Interrupted, Susanna Kaysen.

Giving Up the Ghost: A Memoir, Hilary Mantel. Mantel is the winner of two subsequent Booker prizes for fiction.

The Glass Castle: A Memoir, Jeannette Walls.
One of the best opening paragraphs ever.

The Hare with Amber Eyes: A Hidden Inheritance,
Edmund de Waal.

A Heartbreaking Work of Staggering Genius, Dave
Eggers.

Just Kids, Patti Smith.
Beautifully written.

The Kiss: A Memoir, Kathryn Harrison.
An excruciating story of incest, also beautifully
written.

Lake Wobegon Days, Garrison Keillor.
Gentle humour.

Learning to Drive: And Other Life Stories, Katha Pollitt.

Let's Take the Long Way Home: A Memoir of Friendship,
Gail Caldwell.

The Liars' Club: A Memoir, Mary Karr.
Dealing with a crazy family without self-pity.

Little Failure: A Memoir, Gary Shteyngart.

*A Long Walk to Freedom: The Autobiography of Nelson
Mandela*, Nelson Mandela.

Losing Mum and Pup: A Memoir, Christopher Buckley

Lucky: A Memoir, Alice Sebold.

Maus: A Survivor's Tale, Art Spiegelman.
   A graphic memoir.

McSorley's Wonderful Saloon, Joseph Mitchell.
   Mitchell is not a memoirist, but is a stunning
   non-fiction writer.

The Memory Chalet, Tony Judt.

A Million Little Pieces, James Frey.
   See what the controversy was about.

A Moveable Feast, Ernest Hemingway.

My Childhood, Maxim Gorky.

My Family and Other Animals, Gerald Durrell.

Mystery and Manners: Occasional Prose, Flannery
   O'Connor.

Night, Elie Wiesel.

Out of Africa, Isak Dinesen.

Paris to the Moon, Adam Gopnik.

Pentimento, Lillian Hellman.

Pilgrim at Tinker Creek, Annie Dillard.

The Road from Coorain, Jill Ker Conway.
   Getting out of Australia.

Speak, Memory: An Autobiography Revisited, Vladimir
   Nabokov.
   A classic.

Them: A Memoir of Parents, Francine du Plessix Gray.

This Boy: A Memoir of a Childhood, Alan Johnson.

This Boy's Life: A Memoir, Tobias Wolff.

Uncle Tungsten: Memories of a Chemical Boyhood,
Oliver Sacks.

A Very Easy Death, Simone de Beauvoir.

Wait Till Next Year: A Memoir, Doris Kearns Goodwin.
Her family and the Brooklyn Dodgers.

A Walker in the City, Alfred Kazin.

Wave, Sonali Deraniyagala.
A masterpiece of restraint in the face of enormous
grief.

West with the Night, Beryl Markham and Sara Wheeler.
Stunning prose.

*What I Talk About When I Talk About Running: A
Memoir*, Haruki Murakami.

Why Be Happy When You Could Be Normal? Jeanette
Winterson.
A memoir telling the true story behind her first novel,
Oranges Are Not the Only Fruit.

A Widow's Story: A Memoir, Joyce Carol Oates

Wordstruck: Memoirs, Robert MacNeil.

Writing Home, Alan Bennett.

The Year of Magical Thinking, Joan Didion.

Amazing—some think superhuman—restraint.

Also the work of W. G. Sebald and the bestselling "autobiographical novels" of the Norwegian Karl Ove Knausgaard, which don't fit into any category.

And one day, maybe your book. Books. Why not? See you on the shelves.

About the Author

Beth Kaplan, who was a professional actress in her twenties, left the stage at thirty to earn an MFA in Creative Writing at University of British Columbia. She has taught memoir and personal essay writing at Ryerson University since 1994 and since 2007 also at the University of Toronto, where recently she was given the Excellence in Teaching Award. Her own personal essays have appeared in newspapers and magazines and on CBC Radio. She is the author of *Finding the Jewish*

Shakespeare: The Life and Legacy of Jacob Gordin, a biography of her great-grandfather, and the Sixties memoir *All My Loving: Coming of Age with Paul McCartney in Paris*. Follow Beth's blog at:

www.bethkaplan.ca
www.elizabethkaplan.blogspot.com

If you'd like to contact Beth, to read her blog or some of her own essays or her books, to find out about classes or her services as an editor and writing coach, or to send feedback on this book, please go to her website www.bethkaplan.ca.

I believe in yesterday.

PAUL MCCARTNEY

So do I, dear Paul. So do I.

CPSIA information can be obtained at www.ICGtesting.com
Printed in the USA
LVOW07s1148200814

400074LV00001B/114/P

9 781927 483909